WHEN LOVE BREAKS THROUGH

Kimberly R. Sokoloshy (signature)

WHEN LOVE BREAKS THROUGH
Copyright © 2021 by Kimberly R. Sokolofsky

While any stories in this book are true, some names and identifying information may have been changed to protect the privacy of individuals.

All rights reserved. No part of this book may be reproduced or used in any manner without written permission of the copyright owner except for the use of quotations in a book review. For more information, address: whenlovebreaksthrough@gmail.com.

First paperback edition December 2021

Cover Illustrators: Paul and Luke Sokolofsky
Editor: Melissa Reardon

ISBN 979-8-7150-0879-4 (paperback)
Library of Congress Control Number 2021923289

CONTENTS

INNER SKEPTIC 7

A TRIP TO REMEMBER 10

SELFLESS 13

CALM 17

A LETTER FROM GOD 20

LITTLE MOMENTS 25

APPLE PIES 27

TOY STORY 29

A HOSPICE PARTY 33

OUR SIGN 38

QUESTIONS 40

THE CHRISTMAS GIFT 42

FRAUD 46

WORDS FROM HEAVEN 49

DON'T DIE 56

NEW BEGINNINGS 57

THE UNDERTAKER 65

WHEN THE CLOCK STRIKES 68

DINNERTIME IN PENNSYLVANIA 71

DINNERTIME IN LOCKPORT, NY 74

GROCERY SHOPPING	76
SHOES	78
THE MAN BY THE CASKET	80
MORE EARRINGS	84
PICTURES	87
ACROSS FAITH	89
SEWING MEMORIES	92
COINS	94
A TOUCH FROM HEAVEN	96
COMING THROUGH	99
FINDING HOPE	104
FINCHES	108
AND MORE FINCHES...	111
WHALE-WATCHING FLOP	114
A LITTLE BIT OF THEM ALL	117
GRANDMA DOTTIE	121
TWO LITTLE GIFTS	125
DATA	133

For my incredible mom

Glenda R. Reardon

Forever grateful for the countless ways you have shown

Love always wins.

Inner Skeptic

I am not a writer. In fact, the very sound of "I" and "writer" together in a sentence makes me very uncomfortable. The idea to write never crossed my mind until The Story unfolded. If someone told me I'd be writing a book, I would have laughed out loud and said something like "Me? Now *that* is funny. You are hilarious." I may have gone on explaining why the idea was so ridiculous, insisting the only thing I could possibly write about would be something along the lines of how to make dinner while simultaneously helping three kids with their homework, all while doing the dishes from the night before. No, I didn't plan to write, but little did I know a story would be handed to me that needed to be shared.

This is a story I wish I didn't have, but somehow it is also a story I am incredibly thankful for. Part of this story was my worst, most heartbreaking nightmare. Part of it was beautiful. Another part of it, I never knew was possible. I am sure I wouldn't have believed it myself if someone told it to me. There is a natural skeptic that thrives inside of me, questioning, analyzing, and seeking evidence. Show me the research, show me the numbers, and then I might consider thinking about it. I've heard stories before about spiritual encounters; people dying and experiencing heaven, visions of Jesus, unexplainable events, etc. My initial response had always been to put them in a compartment of my brain labeled "I'll believe it when I see it" and forget about them. I think this is what drew me to a career in Behavior Therapy, specifically Applied Behavior Analysis. This field is a science, and everything is backed by research. Science asks questions that put my skeptic brain at ease: How accurate are the measurements? Does this occur across settings and across people? Can you expect it to occur again?

    After the first event of The Story, my thriving skeptic hung tight to these questions and used them as evidence against the case to take a risk. Despite the awe factor my family had all experienced, I needed more. I needed data…I needed good, undeniable data.

    Then it happened, and not just once. It happened time and again. The impossible happened across people, across time, and across settings. Best of all in my mind, it happened across faiths. The unexplainable occurring over and over again.

    I knew The Story needed to be told. It was too big, too real, and wasn't just for my family to hang on to and cherish. It seemed that God was making quite the effort for The Story to be shared. I still had a question though: why was it given to *me*? Despite all the hours I rationalized to myself and to my husband about why I could not possibly write, every time I desperately tried to swim against the current, I was consistently pulled in the other direction. Sometimes it was a comment from a friend, a note from my husband, a paragraph in a book, a lost earring, or a swarm of yellow finches (to be explained later), and then it was the voice in my head every time I went to work, "Alert! Wrong again! This is not what you are supposed to be doing today. Turn around and write."

    My long, desperate battle to stay on my planned course eventually lost and God's persistence won; I needed to write. Saying this out loud made me feel completely exposed and incredibly vulnerable, like I was suddenly transported out of my shower and into our local grocery store, soaking wet and completely naked. I wanted to hide and cover up quickly every time I mumbled my idea to anyone. I had no clue how to even begin writing a book and no proven evidence that I was gifted enough to actually do it.

    To top off my list of uncertainties, The Story given to me involves faith and Christianity. This sent my mind into a vicious spiral of self-doubt. "Kim, umm, sorry to say, but you are not qualified to write this. You barely know what you believe. You still have questions you wrestle with daily. Kim, the idea is ridiculous." The list went on. My faith was a rollercoaster, with more loops and twists than straight paths. I had spent many years questioning

Christianity, God, and the church, and had felt comfort in my known skepticism. It allowed me to not have to agree with everything, to ask the many questions I had, admit when I didn't get it, and continue to learn. It also didn't classify me in a group of people that honestly, I didn't want to be recognized with. Unfortunately, from a lot of what I had seen of Christians, I didn't want to be considered a part of it. Staying on the skeptic fence felt much safer.

In the last several years though following the start of The Story, I have come to know a different kind of Christianity than I had experienced before. Instead of faith based out of fear, it is faith based in love. Instead of faith based in judgment, this Christianity is based in grace. Instead of a distant God, it's a personal God. Instead of God's love being earned by performance, God's love is free and unconditional. This I could be a part of. I began to understand that God doesn't just want people who are "qualified," and in fact, in some cases, unqualified is even better.

Now, I sit writing The Story that was not in my plans, and about as far as I can get out of my comfort zone. The Story began on December 28, 2013, and continued throughout the next several years. Every now and then we are given another piece to add years later. I expected this story to be only one event, which even by itself was incredible. God, however, must know how stubborn I am. It quickly turned from one unexplainable event with a small group of people, to numerous events across people. It's a story of miracles, of the unexplainable, of a personal God. It's a glimpse into some of the many questions about life after death. It is a real-life account, filled with many data points showing one consistent conclusion...death is *not* the end.

A Trip to Remember

July 2013

Then...Always say yes to a trip, you never know what you are going to see and experience.

Now...Always say yes to a trip, you never know which memories you will cling tightly to forever.

The sun was almost completely down when we pulled into a parking area of Grand Teton National Park. This overlook was known as the spot to see grizzlies, filling their bellies before darkness fell. We looked out of our windows and saw a mother grizzly and her cub, peacefully eating with little regard to all who stopped to watch. As soon as our car was parked, we raced out with our cameras ready. The moment we opened the car door though, all excitement was abruptly halted. We became completely engulfed by a cloud of mosquitoes—bloodsuckers like we had never experienced before. They buzzed ferociously in our ears, flew right into our mouths, and even up our noses. There were seven of us that had hopped out of the car, and five jumped immediately back in. Cornered in the car, they then spent the next couple of minutes declaring war on the hundred or so unrelenting mosquitoes that had seeped into the car just during the two seconds the door had been open.

My mom and I though...we were wildlife freaks. We couldn't pass up a great photo and were determined to capture the majestic scene that somehow went unphased amidst the mosquito inferno. Taking a picture, however, meant you had to stand still, and standing still meant donating your blood to the vicious bloodsuckers that would leave you itching for days. In order to not become completely eaten alive, my mom and I proceeded to do something along the lines of a dance. It was filled with bizarre movements that involved jumping up and down, flapping our arms, swatting our heads, and continuously moving. I surrendered before her and sprinted back to the car with a swarm surrounding me. Inside the car, my three boys and my dad were all laughing hysterically. They had not been watching the bears or the moose that entered the scene, but instead had been much more entertained by my mom and I. I looked out to witness the performance they had been watching. My mom was now entirely alone, doing the most ridiculous dance imaginable in front of at least 20 cars full of people who had chosen to remain mosquito-free. I cannot be sure, but I would bet we were not the only people no longer watching the bears. My mom though, even if she knew the spectacle she was creating, would not have been embarrassed one bit. She lived in the moment, and this was one she wanted to capture.

    The next day we drove to Yellowstone National Park to spend several days experiencing our wondrous earth close-up. We hiked to hot springs, geysers, mud pots, lakes, and waterfalls. We saw elk, grizzlies, wolves, bison, and mountain goats. Our days were filled with awe as we took in the scenes around us. One morning we drove to our favorite valley viewing area to watch for wildlife. We brought our camp stove and pancake mix and made chocolate chip pancakes for all of the other wildlife lovers there. This, to me, was life at its finest. First, I was surrounded by nature which is definitely my happy place. Second, we were able to be generous to strangers, even in the middle of a vacation. Last but not least, I was surrounded by the people I loved most, including my mom, who had just battled cancer a few years earlier and won. Life was good, and gratitude overflowed my soul.

    A few days before we left to return home, we took an evening walk around the geysers to see which ones were set to erupt. As we strolled the boardwalks, a stranger passing by urged us to come quickly, pointing us to adjacent geysers that, in a rare display, were about to explode simultaneously. We followed him to a far section of the boardwalk where 30 people who coined themselves "geyser geeks" stood to watch this momentous event. As my husband, Paul, and I and the boys settled into a good viewing spot, I turned around and realized my parents were no longer with us. I spotted them a ways back, sitting on a bench. Knowing this would typically be something they would rush right along with us to see, I knew something was wrong. My mom showed me her leg, which had suddenly swollen from the knee down. Considering maybe she had been bitten by something, they decided to head to the emergency clinic near the hotel. I returned to my boys to watch the geysers, with no worries of a swollen leg being anything more than that. The geysers exploded as predicted, and they were, of course, spectacular.

    My parents returned shortly after the explosive display and reported the medical staff had given my mom Benadryl, but instructed she get it checked out upon returning home. The boys immediately broke into the conversation with excitement, sharing every detail their grandparents had missed.

    My mom was happy for the change of conversation, as the last thing she wanted was anything weighing her or anyone else down, especially on a trip. She had this constant beam of positivity flowing out of her, so much so that it was typically shocking to people and sometimes just straight-up hilarious. There were several times when we would test her positivity just for fun. We would ask her something like, "Hey Mom, do you want to go out for dinner at that new restaurant you love?" She would enthusiastically say yes and what a great idea that was. In the same breath, someone would propose, "actually let's just have leftovers and do the laundry," and she would legitimately be just as agreeable and excited at the alternative. No, there was no way she would let a little swollen leg steal her joy. We followed her lead and went on with the last couple days of our trip like normal, having tons of fun and making more memories, not knowing that this minor ailment was our first sign of anything but normal.

Selfless

September 27, 2013

Then... I feared death like some people fear heights or snakes. The thought of death for myself, my family, or my loved ones was more than I could handle, so I tried hard to avoid even thinking about it. It brought nothing but horribly sad, confusing, fear-filled thoughts.

Now... What if it's possible for love to overcome pain, even the worst kind imaginable—even death?

The phone rang. It was the sound I had hoped to hear several hours ago, but the wait turned my hope into dread. As each hour, minute, and then second passed, the anticipation had become unbearable. My imagination had transformed into my own worst enemy, conjuring up nightmarish stories of what could have caused this long delay. Every extra minute made my greatest fear seem closer to reality. After hours of impatiently waiting, the last thing I wanted to do was pick up the phone.

Earlier that morning, I had already figured it out for myself. My mom just had some weird infection that a heavy dose of antibiotics would clear up in a few days. She would be down to visit in two weeks, if that. She'd be playing baseball with the boys and making chocolate chip pancakes like usual. We'd even go on a nice hike, laughing the whole way up the mountain at how nervous we got over a wimpy, minor infection. The swollen leg had gotten better, and surely this new symptom would too.

My pleasant little explanation was apparently crushed by

the time I reached for the phone, as my hand trembled so incessantly that I could hardly press the button to answer. As much as I wanted my simple diagnosis to be true, I knew it wouldn't take this long to prescribe a few pills.

    I finally answered, and stepped outside onto our patio, closing the door behind me. I did not want the boys around in case the worst-case scenario was reality. I attempted to mask my fear-filled voice as I presented a nonchalant "hello" into the phone. I did not want my mom to get any hint of the awful, negative path my mind had gone down in the last few hours. I was struck immediately by the sound of *both* of them on the other line. Thoughts streamed from my heart to my mind… "No, please no! Oh no, this is bad. This is really bad. Why would *both* of them be on the line? No!" I wanted to hang up. I wanted to stop the clock right there and pause life for eternity. Maybe if I didn't hear it, it wouldn't actually be true? Before I could get another word out, my mom spoke. She spoke calmly and lovingly. She spoke the two words I feared most. "It's cancer."

    I took it in only for a split second and spit it right back out like a rotten tomato. The bitterness lingered in my mouth, but I refused to eat it. "No," I said. "No it's not. Time to laugh and say you are joking. Very funny. You guys are a riot." She tenderly and selflessly responded to my denial. "I'm so sorry honey."

    My heart instantly hurt. She was telling me her cancer was back with a vengeance, and she was mourning for me—for <u>me</u>! My mind swarmed again. How could this be happening to her? A person who endlessly thinks of others before herself and says "I'm sorry" as she announces her own fate. As I fought my welling eyes and the enormous lump in my throat, I attempted to listen to the details only to search for any signs of hope. Maybe surgery, maybe even chemo again, whatever it would take for this not to be true. Instead, the words that were highlighted in my brain were "metastatic," and "stage IV." These words played in my head like a skipping CD, repeating over and over, with increasing intensity. Then I heard it—one word that might at least get me through this conversation—"treatment." I threw myself at that word and clung to it tightly until we hung up. I clung to it as I tried to be optimistic for her, trying to be anywhere close to the selflessness she always modeled. I told her we'd beat it. We beat it last time and now we'd beat it again.

My hand trembled as I slowly hung up and the next thing I knew, the phone went sailing across our backyard and lodged itself into a bush. I begin to scream at the top of my lungs, sobbing and wishing I had more things to throw. My cries were uncontrollable, coming from the greatest depths of me. Sounds came out of me that I had never heard before. I yelled continuously. "Not her, not her! Why, why? God, no. Noooo, dammit NO!"

My husband stood close, and without hearing any details, he knew. He tried to comfort me, but his touch only brought me back to earth, the last place I wanted to be. He didn't say a word, knowing there was nothing, nothing in this moment that could help. So he just stood nearby, head slightly down, processing the awfulness in his own way.

I eventually slid to the ground of my patio and put my head between my knees. My husband held me tightly, attempting to calm my incessant shaking. I tried to breathe, and I remembered my three boys inside watching a show that would soon be over. My heart ached for them more than anything, and the thought of telling them the news was excruciating. She was like their second mom. She was truly a *grand* mom. She was part of them; they were part of her. They needed each other. They loved each other. No, no, no! I took more deep breaths like I was practicing Lamaze. Got to get it together. Got to help them through this too. Got to be like Mom—selfless.

I turned to look into the house and saw my three boys peeking out the sliding glass door. I realized they must have heard and were now wondering if the storm was over and if it was safe to come out. I had completely lost control, and I realized that they must have heard my cries over the television, along with my screams and words they had never heard come out of my mouth.

My husband waved them over, and without a sound, all three walked directly over and put their arms around me. They didn't say a single word, just quietly came only to comfort their mom. They paused all the questions filling their own minds. They paused all the fears they were experiencing as they heard my cries and saw my face red and soaked in tears. My five-, seven-, and nine-year-old children put themselves aside and comforted me. My shaking began to slow as I felt their little arms wrap around me. Then my oldest spoke softly as he pressed his head tightly next to mine, "I'm sorry, Mom," just as my mom had said a few minutes before. I completely lost it again, though this time it wasn't just from the pain I felt. It was from knowing her gift was alive and well...the gift of selfless love she taught them so well.

Calm

October 3, 2013

Then… When shit hits the fan, watch out! It explodes everywhere into a giant disaster, covering everything and everyone in its path.

Now… What if the fan isn't on?

    Just a week after receiving the worst news we could imagine, I made the six-hour drive from Pennsylvania to New York to attend an appointment that would give us answers we were not sure we wanted. We walked through the entrance of Roswell Cancer Center in Buffalo. Though they tried hard to create a light and pleasant atmosphere, including live musicians in the lobby, the place was filled with bald heads, wheelchairs, and ample literature on cancer. No matter how upbeat the music or how many chocolate chip cookies were being offered, no one was happy to be there.

    We opened the doors to the "breast clinic," and every chair was full. The room was packed with so many beautiful women, all different ages, all wondering about their future. We watched woman after woman walk through the doors as her name was called. I couldn't help but wonder what laid beyond this waiting room for them. Would they hear the news they hoped for, or the news they feared the worst?

    I desperately tried to avoid looking at the woman a few seats down, whose skin was yellow and face puffy. Her arm was wrapped in medical tape and she sat in a wheelchair. Despite all the effects of the cancer, it was obvious she was younger than a lot of the others, maybe in her 30s. A man who appeared to be her husband sat next to her, hand in hand. I wondered how much time she had left. I fought all the painful questions that came to my mind. Will my mom look like this soon? Will someone else be looking at us one day wondering these very same questions, and if so, what will be the answer? A few years, a few months, days?

I stopped there in my downward spiral and tried to focus on my mom instead, who looked well, hair and everything. In fact, she looked healthier than most of the other people there.

"Glenda?" The nurse called. We got up quickly but cautiously, aware of the conversation that hid behind the next door. As I followed my parents into the room, I tried to convince myself to be hopeful and positive. Maybe Stage IV wasn't that bad, maybe there was surgery or chemo again…maybe there was something.

As soon as the doctor said his first word, my attempts at positivity were destroyed quicker than a block tower in front of a two-year-old. His tone was serious and his words were bleak. "Your cancer has spread, Glenda—all over," he said. "It's a mess in there. You can try chemo if you decide, but you need to take quality of life into account for the time you have left."

A mess?!! Quality of life?!! Time you have left?!!! My head screamed…YOU ARE A DOCTOR! YOU HAVE TO DO MORE THAN THIS! WHO ARE YOU TO TALK LIKE THIS? THERE HAS TO BE BETTER OPTIONS! YOU NEED TO FIX HER DAMMIT! I pictured myself standing up and screaming this, making the doctor understand his words were just not acceptable.

Instead, I turned toward my mom, looking for camaraderie for the eminent verbal attack of this doctor. When I saw her face, however, the train wreck I was about to embark on came to a sudden halt. I stared at her, completely marveled by her calmness. Barely moving, she was almost nodding in agreement with him. I screamed in my head as if she could hear me without saying anything, "Mom, don't you hear what he is telling you?" I decided she must not have understood what he was saying. But then she asked him a question, and it was clear she was on track. She had heard. She listened as he responded, shaking his head and saying he wished there was better news. "Hmm," she said, taking it all in. "Hmm," she said, in just the same way as when asked a question like what should we have for dinner, or what card game do you want to play?

Part of me still wanted to scream, but the other part was even more fixated on my mom. He was telling her she was going to die. He was shaking his head and saying words like "prognosis," "quality of life," etc. Somehow though, she had an uncanny peace about her, like there was nothing that could break her or her spirit. Not cancer, not even death. I felt fear and strength all at the same time. I looked at her, facing death right in the eye, and I felt prouder of her than ever.

Then the grief struck me again and shattered everything positive I had just been feeling. I looked away, holding back tears, thinking "not her, not her, not her! Not my mom." I didn't want her to see my fear or the way my heart had just been shattered. I focused hard on her courage, hoping some of it would carry over to me. It worked for a moment and I turned again to see her. She was looking at me with a calm but questioning look, as if to ask, "I think I heard him right. Not good, not good at all. Did you hear the same thing?" I took a deep breath as we kept our eyes locked, her calm and strength cradling the broken pieces of my heart, then I nodded my head slowly. "Yes, Mom, yes. We are on the same page."

I looked away and realized it was clear, this is how we were going to handle this disaster. We would handle it with the same love, patience, gentleness, and grace as she always demonstrated. This situation, even facing death itself, would be no different.

A Letter from God

October 29, 2013

Then…Is God personal? Is God even real? If so, why wouldn't he save my mom of all people? She's selfless, full of unconditional love, and overflowing with joy. If you are real, God, why would you let this happen?

Now…Answers to these questions are not black and white, and no matter how many people you ask, they will each have a different answer. Sometimes things are felt or experienced much more than they can be explained.

    I had spent the last few days at home anxiously awaiting our next trip to New York. It had been one week since I had seen my mom, which seemed like an eternity now. Time was no longer a given. Time was precious. We went the week before to the Cleveland Clinic in Ohio to get a second opinion, hoping the doctor there would have some magical treatment that Roswell did not. Though he was gentle and thoughtful in his wording, his prognosis was the same.
    The kids were finishing their week in school, and I tried to stay positive while I impatiently waited. I had everything cleaned and packed days before, even though I typically would procrastinate and pack the night before. I decided to go for a run to try to settle my brain and heart as I counted the minutes until we could get back to my mom. With each step of my run, I began to wrestle with God more and more. I was doubting everything I believed.
    Step… I had just started to actually believe in a loving

God, but would a loving God let my mom die?
    Step…Maybe this whole God thing is actually bogus?
    Step…Did I let myself get brainwashed somehow into some made-up religion?
    Step…How did I get suckered into believing God truly cared about each person?
    Step…How could I have believed that God loved each one of us, including my mom?
    Step…If he did really love her, why would this be happening?
    Step…I prayed for a miracle every day, and everyone I knew was praying too—and nothing. No healing, no miracles.
    Step…Instead, she is only getting worse.
    Step…If you are real God, where are you now?

    These thoughts and running began to not mix well. I was heading up a hill and already short of breath, with rage boiling inside and tears pouring down my face. I couldn't catch my breath. Air would only enter my mouth and come right back out like there was a barricade blocking its way. I didn't want to stop running though; I was trying to run off the pain inside. I had never hyperventilated before, but there's a first for everything. I thought passing out might be okay, maybe even pleasant versus my current tormented state.

    A friend happened to be driving by, right as I reached the crest of the hill. I stopped running and tried to get myself together, hoping she wouldn't notice that I was about 20 seconds from falling flat on my face. She slowed for a moment, saying something about how she had heard my mom's cancer was back and how sorry she was. I took my first actual breath and mustered up a thank you and she kept driving.

    My torment continued, but at least now I was able to breathe. My questions about God and to God continued. After I got home and calmed down a bit, I called my mom to check in. The moment I heard her voice, a thought hit me. She must have these questions too. We have always thought and felt very similarly. I didn't want her to think any of these thoughts I just had. Not now. I didn't want her to think she was abandoned, to feel like God didn't love her, or that she was forgotten. To feel like maybe God wasn't even real. To think that maybe this is just the dark and dreary end. I didn't want her to think this, because truly, even though I was angry and devastated, it's not what I believed. I did still believe God loved her. I believed he somehow thought she was even more amazing than I did. I believed God knew her and cared about each thing she was going through. Although I didn't know the answer to many questions about God, I believed that God was with her from day one and even beyond this earthly end, through all the beauty and all the pain. I wanted her to know this.

After throwing punches at God just an hour before, I felt for one of the first times in my life, God was asking me to do something. It was something he needed me to do for her, his daughter that he loved—something that would be out of my comfort zone, which was putting on paper what I thought was true and then sharing that with my mom. Our family never really talked about faith together, nothing more than a standard scripted prayer at dinner. This would be new, and quite possibly awkward, but I no longer had time to waste holding something in because it might be uncomfortable. I sat down and, in 30 minutes, wrote a letter to my mom about what I thought God would say to her.

Dear my beloved daughter Glenda,

You are everything I have hoped for, perfect just the way you are. Your beauty shows from the inside out. I know so many who have been touched by your kind, loving spirit, thank you for that.

I remember you in the fun, old days on the farm, running in the dirt, picking up worms, cooking for others with your mom, and late nights playing cards. I can even remember your kindness back then. When most kids became defiant and ungrateful, you stayed you. Glenda, I was so proud. Not everything was easy, but you were always able to see the bright side. You didn't know at the time, but both the kindness and toughness you gained in your childhood would be well used in your future.

Glenda, I was with you when your father died, on that sad, dark day. Wow, how he loves you. He knows, like I do, how very special you are. I loved watching you and John fall in love and build your beautiful family. You are an amazing, loving mom and have taught your children what unconditional love looks like. They are very thankful for that. Whew, parenting wasn't always easy though. I remember the day I sent the doctor to quickly save your son, and the storm to save your daughter. You, and they, were not alone. Your faith and your loving, optimistic personality carried you through.

Do you remember the story of Mary and Martha? Glenda, you remind me so much of Mary. You always take the time to be fully present with people and give them all the love you have to offer. You welcome people with open arms and they feel your genuine, caring heart when you are with them. You are always able to put people as your top priority and understand the rest will come (that is something some people never learn). Your joy of life is absolutely contagious and you have, and will continue to, share that with many.

Glenda, I know what you are going through now, and I am with you in this. It pains me as much as it pains you. Cancer is ugly, awful, evil, and I hate it as much as you do. You are such a beloved daughter of mine, and it hurts me that you are going through this. There is so much good in the world, but evil still exists. Please know that I did not cause this to happen but trust I will make good from it. This will not be easy to see, especially on the darkest days. Trust that as in your past, beautiful things can grow from the worst.

Glenda, your time here is not over, and for that matter, it will never be over. Your joy, positivity, love, and faith have been passed on to so many already and will carry on through generations. When one day you do come to live for eternity with me, your impact will last and your loving spirit will never end, like an angel in heaven and earth.

For now, your time here is not done. I have more for you yet, more joyous moments to be had. You have more games of cards to play with your grandkids, more great laughs to be had. You are an amazing grandma to those cute grandchildren of yours. I have loved watching your relationship with each of them grow, and they each will be very grateful for every moment they have with their special grandmother. You are very loved and cherished.

In the meantime, trust that I am with you each and every day. I know this can be very hard to see, as I'm known to be pretty elusive sometimes. I will give you many more moments of peace, love, and joy, and will also be there in the worst of it—in the pain, the fears, the loneliness, the doubts. My spirit surrounds you; you are not alone! You are completely, unconditionally loved, my beautiful daughter, and I will always be right by your side.

In presence,
God

After I finished writing, I realized I wouldn't be able to read this to my mom without bawling my eyes out. So, since I had already cried myself dry for 30 minutes straight while writing the letter, I washed my face, put on some makeup to cover my swollen eyes, and videotaped myself reading it.

When we arrived at my parent's house later that night, I showed her the video and gave her the letter. She smiled and cried as she took it all in.

When it was over, she looked at me and asked, "Do you believe this, Kimberly? Do you believe it's all true?"

I shook my head yes, and replied, "Yes, mom, I do. Every bit of it."

She nodded and told me how beautiful it was, and I told her I believed it was what God wanted her to know. Then, for the first time any of us verbalized the fact that she was dying, that this time she was not going to be saved despite all of the painful treatments, all of our prayers, all of our hope, she turned to me and said, "I'd like you to read this letter at my funeral. I think it needs to be shared."

Little Moments

November 26, 2013

Then...Cherishing the big moments is easy. Small, everyday moments, however, quickly are forgotten.

Now...What if the moment right in front of you is a moment to treasure, no matter how ordinary it seems, no matter how frequently you do it?

    My mom and I shopped together often and always before Christmas. We spent many hours walking through aisles, discussing what each family member needed or what they would like. We examined each potential gift and gave each other the nod of approval, or the look of "you must be joking, right?" We would often stop for lunch in the middle of a long day of shopping to refuel for the hours ahead. This year, given the impending doom we faced, we decided to start our shopping earlier than usual.
    Mom had been feeling pretty good today. She got ready, though a little slower than usual, and put on a hat to cover her once again bald head. She wrapped her PICC line carefully to prevent infection. The PICC line ran directly into her bloodstream to provide her the nourishment she needed since the cancer blocked her stomach from performing its function. My dad was perplexed that we would even think about shopping considering her condition and the potential risks, but thankfully the patient calls the shots.
    I didn't buy much, as I was really only focused on helping with her gifts. It didn't matter at all what the gifts were, it only

mattered that they were from her. Anyone lucky enough to get a handpicked gift from her this year would treasure it, no matter how big or small.

    Her gifts though were thoughtful as always. She picked out one for each grandchild, including a book with a truck on it for my nephew and an extra soft blanket for my five-year-old who loved cozy things. We talked about the items, she told me about her thoughts for each one, and she continued to shop, determined as usual to find gifts for the people she loved.

    As I watched her thoughtfully choose each item, I found myself stepping away slightly, moving behind a row of books to take a few deep breaths. I didn't want to ruin the moment, but the thoughts flooded in despite my best efforts to stay positive.

    These gifts would likely be her last. This shopping trip would likely be our last. These little moments I typically took for granted would soon be the very moments I would do anything for—anything to have just one more.

Apple Pies

November 28, 2013

Then….Nobody can make an apple pie as good as my mom.

Now….Nobody can make an apple pie as good as my mom.

    Food, food, and more food. My mom loved to cook, and we all loved her cooking. This Thanksgiving, homemade pies lined the counter as usual, delicious smells flowed into each room, and a picturesque turkey was taken out of the oven. Family filed into the dining room, one after the next, ready to enjoy the feast. All of us sat hungry and ready to enjoy, all except for Betty Crocker herself. Instead, my mom sat at the table with us, tube in her arm, pumping in the same nutrients from a bag that we were getting from our food.
    I couldn't think of a more ironic arrangement. My mom has spent her life as a mom, wife, and dietician, teaching people about nutrition, cooking healthy food, and creating recipes. Now she sat at what would likely be her last Thanksgiving—unable to eat. She is a person who would cook three different meals for breakfast, one for each picky child, and could feed 20 people with just a 20 minutes notice. Now, she chose to just sit with us and watch, fighting the nausea that strong smells brought, determined just to be with us. We all ate our meal as quickly as we could, equally determined not to make her symptoms even worse.
    The night before, my husband had asked my mom to teach him how to make her apple pie. She happily obliged, telling

him step by step what to do, and picking on him as usual when he messed up. When the pie was done, she was obviously proud of him and jokingly let him know. "Wow, Paul, I didn't know you could cook!" Though she could not taste it, she assured him it was a job well done. I watched them go back and forth, jabbing at each other as he lovingly assumed one of her previous roles. I couldn't help fight back tears, wondering when this would become the new norm: Paul, the baker of mom's apple pies.

Toy Story

December 15, 2013

Then…How could a kid possibly process all of this—terminal cancer, death, grief, anger, hope, denial?

Now…Probably better than adults.

    My oldest son, Jake, is only nine years old and is the most insightful, perceptive person I have ever known. He understands things that would surpass the capacity of many adults, including me. Usually, we have seen this as a gift. During tense, difficult situations though, this can be challenging for him and for us. He senses the deepest feelings of others, even the feelings we'd like to protect him from.
    The past week had been a living nightmare, and he had experienced the worst of it. My husband and I decided to let him come with me for the six-hour drive to New York, as my mom had just been admitted to intensive care. Her cancer had suddenly taken an ugly, violent, painful turn. Jake overheard my conversation with Paul that I would be going to see her and insisted with every ounce of audacity and love he had in him that he would come as well. We attempted to discourage him, but his mind was set. Jake was wise beyond his years and felt the weight of the situation as much as we did. He didn't want to miss any chance to be with her, sick or not. So, hesitantly, we allowed him to come, hoping that if nothing else, his presence would bring some light and joy to her hospital room.

We spent the next few days in the hospital; long, 12-hour days. Doctors and nurses buzzed in and out of his grandma's room constantly. My dad and I took excruciating phone calls in front of him updating family, each one delivering more bad news. All of this was happening with grandma sick in the middle of it, in severe pain, vomiting off and on, an extremely uncomfortable tube up her nose draining her stomach, and her color turning more and more yellow each day. All of the physical pain was topped with maybe an even more stabbing emotional pain, her desperate desire to get home with the grim realization that she could not.

Jake sang her songs she had taught him and rubbed her feet with lotion attempting to distract her from the pain, as my dad and I met outside the room with a team of doctors to hear the worst news: there was no getting better now. Hospice would be coming to meet with us and offering heavy pain medications to help her through to the end.

Outside of her hospital room, my dad resembled a walking zombie. He tried hard to keep it together in front of her, but grief followed him like a dark shadow everywhere he went. Jake watched him out of the corner of his eye as he jumped between periods of utter sadness, deep anger, disbelief, and fear. Jake, nor I, had ever experienced or witnessed grief like this. Jake would watch as grandpa broke down into uncontrollable periods of crying or stared off to nowhere, detached from anything going on around him.

Within a couple days, my husband and our other two boys joined us in New York, knowing the severity of her condition. After another long day in the hospital for us all, we headed to my parent's house to put the boys to bed. My mom had been anticipating countless fun, grandkid-filled weekends in their new house, and had designed a room just two months prior that would feel like a second home to them.

Jake stopped my husband and I in the hallway before heading into the bedroom and said steadily, "Mom and dad, can I ask you something?"

"Of course, buddy, go for it," I replied.

"Remember the movie *Toy Story 3*? You know the part when Lotsa, that big bear, gets lost and eventually finds his way home, but when he gets home he sees that his owner has already replaced him?"

"Yea, Jake, I remember that part." My husband and I glanced at each other, an idea in our heads as to where this conversation was going.

"Well, they said in the movie that when that happened to him, something was lost inside of him that he would never get back."

My heart dropped. Yep, he was heading where I feared he might.

"Lotsa turned mean and lonely and was never happy again. Is that what is going to happen to grandpa?"

My husband and I stood motionless and stunned, so Jake continued.

"Is he going to lose something when grandma dies?" His words got quieter and a tear rolled down his cheek. "And then we lose grandpa too?" he asked.

Tears poured out of him now as his last sentence came out. Paul and I wrapped him in our arms and hugged him tightly. All I could get out at first was, "you are amazing Jake." We continued to hug him as we bought time to process what he just said. He was waiting for more of a response than just a compliment on his intellectual ability.

Eventually getting our heads together, we responded, "No buddy, we are not going to let that happen."

"How?" He sounded doubtful. "What can we do to help him?"

"Jake, in that movie, Lotsa is alone and has no one there to love him after his owner doesn't want him anymore. Grandpa is not alone. We are all still here, and we love him a ton. Lotsa doesn't have anyone, and he doesn't have love. We are not going to let that happen to grandpa, because we are never going to stop loving him. The love he feels isn't only from grandma, buddy, it's from all of us."

We hugged him even tighter and held him for a while, Paul and I catching eyes every now and then, wondering what to do next. Here was our nine-year-old son, relating a movie to this real-life situation. He feared that not only was he losing his beloved grandma to cancer, but that he would also lose his beloved grandpa to grief. He could see the way that grandpa had been drifting away in the past couple of weeks and wondered if something would die inside grandpa that he would never get back.

As we tucked Jake into bed and kissed him goodnight, I prayed the response I gave Jake was true. I prayed that his grandpa, my dad, would not end up like Lotsa. I prayed that love would be the winner in this story.

A Hospice Party

December 18, 2013

Then…How much is God really a part of our earthly lives? How do we know what's from God, and what's from us?

Now…When there's no explanation, when there's beauty in the most unexpected place, when love beats the worst pain: that's God.

    The family room of the hospice house was completely packed. People lined the walls, pouring over into the hallway, and every seat was taken. The room had been temporarily transformed into a place of celebration for what we were calling a "retirement party." Congratulations banners were hung. A large quilt was laid out for all guests to sign. A giant cake sat on the table, surrounded by mounds of other party food. Music along with a slideshow of pictures of my mom's life played in the background. Although it was her official day of retirement from her career of 29 years as a dietitian, everyone there knew what the party really was. It was their last chance to see her, to tell her she is amazing, to tell her how she has touched their lives. For many of them, it was their last chance to say goodbye.
    My mom had asked for this party a couple of weeks prior, before her cancer took a sharp turn for the worse. We knew planning anything at this stage would be risky, as every day her condition changed drastically. One moment she would be up playing games with the boys, sharing about her childhood, and the next she'd be in pain and exhausted. We desperately wanted to

grant every wish we possibly could though, and this party was something she was not willing to let go. She boundlessly loved people and cared for each person that was lucky enough to get to know her. To my mom, the risk of all these people coming and not even being able to see her was better than not inviting them at all. Her positive spirit wasn't overtaken by the cancer, and she declared that she would be fine for the party. We declared we would do everything we could to make her wish come true.

When the morning of the party came, however, I walked into her room at Hospice to see my dad shaking his head. She had woken up violently vomiting and was in a lot of pain. Ugg.

These last few weeks were nothing but a series of real-life nightmares, and another worst-case scenario was unfolding right before our eyes. She wanted this party so badly, to be surrounded by family, friends, and coworkers, and now her cancer was attempting to strip that pleasure away from her too.

The party was set to start at 4 p.m. After a rough, painful day, she requested a dose of heavy pain meds at 3 p.m. Typically, a dose of this medication would leave her sound asleep for hours, unable to be woken. Now sound asleep, we realized it was too late to cancel the party and that we would have to do the party without her. They could peek in on her sleeping, or just leave her a note. It wouldn't be the same, but it was our only choice.

Five minutes before the start, however, she woke up suddenly from what looked like a solid slumber. She turned to my dad and the first thing she asked was, "What time is it?"

"3:55. Don't worry about it though, hon. You need your rest."

"No," she replied quickly, now fully awake, "Help me up. I have to get dressed."

My dad hesitantly helped her out of bed and into her fancy clothes we had picked out the day before. I helped her with her makeup as she requested, complete with a wig and jewelry. My dad insisted that she didn't need any of that, but she wanted to look as healthy as she possibly could. She wanted to look ready for a party, hospice or not. She was satisfied with the five-minute makeover, and by 4:01 p.m., we wheeled her out the door toward the crowd of people.

There was a steady stream of hugs and smiles and people

holding back tears. Her voice, which had been fading steadily each day, was now remarkably strong. Her nausea and the drowsy effects of the pain medications had somehow vanished. She smiled brightly at each new face she saw, and her positive spirit surprised each person she greeted. "She is still the same positive, happy Glenda," they all remarked. "It just doesn't seem possible that she is in hospice." They had expected to see the exhausted, painful side of terminal cancer—the side that was so present just hours before. Instead, her strength continued throughout the party, allowing her to stand and cut her retirement cake (which she couldn't even eat), to talk, laugh, encourage, and share her love for life with others.

In the middle of the party, my oldest brother, Ryan, got everyone's attention. My mom knew that he and my cousin were going to play a couple of songs she had requested, but he surprised my mom with the first song, "Hallelujah," with lyrics he changed just for her.

The room got quiet, and my mom sat in the center in her wheelchair, surrounded now by over a hundred people in one small room. He started the song and her eyes were glued on him.

"Glenda Rae is a diamond queen, she sometimes comes to me in my dreams, a farmer's daughter so full of love and laughter..."

Her face lit up as she realized he had written this just for her, and a tear dripped down her cheek.

He continued, "I heard that God might be needing you soon, she's missed you so like an angel's tune..."

I had been standing next to my mom but moved in front of her to videotape as she watched. As I started recording, she locked eyes with me and began to cry a cry that I had not yet seen.

I watched her face change as the painful reality set in. She knew in this moment she was really dying. Her face was a mixture of fear and grief. Her eyes stared into mine, and her look said it all. *"This is really happening, isn't it? Oh God... I am dying. I'm scared. I don't want to leave you all, all of this, all of these people. No!"*

Her chin quivered as she continued looking at me. I quickly put down the camera to hug her. I whispered into her ear, "I love you so much, Mom." I caught my breath, fighting to get out my next line. "You are going to be okay Mom. You are going to be so okay." She nodded, knowing as well as me that "okay" did not mean an earthly cure anymore, but that she was going to be forever, way better than "okay."

We stayed with arms around each other as we listened to my brother, and I watched her face as her mind continued to run. I could see that there was another feeling playing wildly in her mind, stronger than the grief or fear—another piece that was just as clear. These difficult but beautiful words sung by my brother were filled with painful truth, but also with words of faith, love, and hope. This party, although not without tears and sadness, overflowed with amazing, overwhelming love.

She smiled through tears as she looked at my brother and then back at me. I could see her thoughts again in her eyes: "*Do you hear this, do you hear his words? Do you see all these people, feel all this love? Your brother is singing a song he wrote just for me, that I will be with God soon. I love you all and I know how much you all love me. I can feel it.*" Her tears flowed heavily.

Tears dripped down my cheeks, my emotions and faith going through flips and turns of their own. The doubt crept in. "God, please, will she really be okay? This whole heaven thing is real right? God, ohhh, please be real." I hoped I was telling her the truth, that she truly was going to be okay. Every bit of me hoped this wasn't some made-up story we humans tell to make ourselves feel better when we die or lose someone. I looked at my grandma, tears dripping steadily at the thought of losing her daughter. I glanced at my dad, with his face also soaked in tears. I felt their pain, their grief, and I doubted every belief in God I thought I had.

I looked at my brother, who was now playing the next song she requested: "I Can Only Imagine," by MercyMe. My brother, who had an agnostic view of spirituality, joined my cousin in performing some very Jesus-centered songs. Typically, Ryan would have chuckled at a request to play a Christian song; it's not his style of music and not his beliefs. But there he was, playing a song of faith, and hoping just like me that each lyric was true, that this was not the end, hoping that she would be forever in the beautiful place that Christians call heaven.

The room was filled with tears. The song was about how amazing the day would be when we first meet Jesus. I looked around at all the people, at the dripping eyes, my mom in the middle of it all, and somehow despite all of this, overwhelming joy filled me. The emotion shocked me. How could I feel joy when we were singing this song about her, about my mom, about her going to heaven? Heaven means gone, right? How could there be joy in this?

The unforeseen feeling continued though. The love in the room was so present it was like you could reach out and touch it. A room full of people who knew and loved my mom, a mixture of Catholics, Protestants, agnostics, and atheists. There were people singing, crying, and smiling as we sang about the incredible love God has for us, and what it will be like when she meets Jesus. Our own personal beliefs were set aside, and hope united us all. Some listened to the lyrics and although they may not have usually believed them, in this moment they hoped each word they were singing was true. Some stood there in trust—trust that each word was real, and that she would live beautifully for eternity.

I looked through the crowd at each of the faces. Tears flowed. Beautiful, loving tears. In their tears, she had given them the gift of love in their life—unconditional love. She had touched them all. That love was potent in the room.

I could not physically hide this feeling anymore, and I began to smile. I looked at my mom sitting in the middle of it all, brightly smiling herself now and singing along, watching this unlikely duet perform. My smile widened and widened until I was almost laughing—almost laughing at a goodbye party for my mom. How could this be?

Then it struck me: this is God, his spirit, right here in the room, an almost tangible spirit—an amazing spirit dispelling the darkness and letting light flow in, at the most unlikely time. I laughed as I thought, of course, this would be God. In the most unexpected, unlikely ways, he shows us that the impossible is actually possible. Beauty in the face of pain, love winning in the face of death.

Our differences disappeared as we stood together in love and hope in that hospice room. This was the God I had been learning about, one who makes beautiful things happen from the worst. The beauty in that room was beyond us. We were not alone. She was not alone. My smile broke open, and I laughed.

Our Sign

December 23, 2013

Then...Signs? Miracles? Likely more of a coincidence. I'm sure it's comforting for people who have lost loved ones to believe in them, but I just can't see it being true.

Now... Signs? Miracles? Still very doubtful. If it were to be true though, if there was any way at all, it'd be something like a bird or a rainbow, not something superficial like an earring.

    I had been sitting by her bed for a while, just watching her as she slept. In the last couple of days since she had been home from the hospice house, even watching her sleep was a gift. At least she was still with us. Since her wish was to be home for her last days, hospice helped make that transition while still giving her the care she needed. They helped to transform the office on the first floor into a completely functioning hospital room, equipped with everything she could possibly need. The house was filled with people, including my dad, brothers, their spouses, children, dogs, as well my family of five. Despite all the commotion thirteen people in one house created, she slept solidly in her bed.

    I realized it was almost noon, so I got up quietly to make lunch for the boys and headed toward the door.

    "Kimberly," she said.

    I stopped in my tracks, surprised by the sound of her voice, and turned around. She was awake.

    "Hey, Mom!"

She smiled at me lovingly and continued quickly, only having very small amounts of energy to even talk now. "I was thinking we need to have a sign."

My heart smiled and cried at the same time. She knew that I would continue to need her, but she also knew her time here was almost up. She knew we may need this "sign" soon. I walked over to hold her hand. Despite my deeply planted skepticism that signs actually happen, in this moment I hoped desperately that somehow it could be true. I knew that if a sign ever really did happen, it would have to be *very* obvious: flashing lights, arrows, and maybe even a label. I didn't want her to know my doubts though. How could I doubt my mother on her literal death bed? So I replied simply, "Yea, Mom, we do."

She then went on steadily, as if she had already given this some thought. "Whenever you lose an earring, know that I am with you. Remember how much I love you. Think about what is going on in your life and what I am trying to tell you."

My first thought was: uhh, an earring? Really? Losing an earring is our sign? First of all, I rarely lose earrings. My mom and I would always give each other earrings for gifts, but I couldn't remember the last time I had lost one. Second of all, shouldn't it be something a little more…natural? Everything I had ever heard about people who claimed to experience signs talked about things like birds or sunset. Plus, anything that happened a little more regularly than losing an earring once every couple of years would be great. An earring seemed like such an unnatural, material thing. If signs are actually real, how can they have anything to do with something worldly?

In just the few seconds it took me to think of other ideas, she dozed back off to sleep. "Mom," I said loudly, but she was already out. I continued to scratch my head, thinking why in the world an earring? I decided that the next time she was awake and alert I would bring it back up so I could change the sign with her. I now had a list of them that I was sure would be much better.

The days went on, however, and there was never another opportunity to bring it up. There was nothing I could do anymore to change it. I accepted that this whole sign thing was highly unlikely anyway and pushed it out of my mind.

Questions

December 24, 2013

Then...All questions need answers.

Now...Maybe some questions can't be answered until we actually experience the answers ourselves.

On Christmas Eve morning, my mom woke up and told me she was scared to die. She said she had a lot of questions and would like to talk to the pastor of our church. She and my dad attended our church regularly since they visited often and had come to know our pastor well. She wanted to know what would happen when she died, what heaven would be like, and if she would still be with us somehow. She said she didn't want to miss seeing the grandkids grow up, and at this, tears began to trickle down her cheeks.

I gave her hand a gentle squeeze and assured her I would get him on the phone with her right away so she could ask him anything she wanted. Within seconds though, she fell back asleep. I tried to wake her, phone now in hand, but she was out. I sat by her side, hoping there would be another day when all these questions could be answered. I wanted her to be able to ask anything she wanted and subside every worry that was brewing in her mind.

As much as I hoped for this to happen though, I also knew there was a good chance it wouldn't. Her times of alertness had been very rare the last few days and having a phone conversation was even more challenging. It was hard enough for us to share even more than a few sentences at this point. I watched her as she slept again, and prayed that in the worst-case scenario, if this conversation was never actually able to happen, somehow her mind would be put at ease. I prayed somehow, in some way, her questions would be answered.

The Christmas Gift

December 25, 2013

Then...Prayer doesn't make any sense and is really kind of weird. If God is all-knowing, doesn't he just know our thoughts and prayers? Why would we even need to pray then?

Now...Prayer is a gift God has given us, both for ourselves, and a gift to give to others.

    A question had been on everyone's mind for many days. We needed to know, but we also did not want to know: would she make it to Christmas? When we had finally gotten the nerve to ask the doctor though, we asked rhetorically, waiting for only one, positive response. He did not play along. Instead, he did the noble doctor thing and told us what he thought was the truth. We painfully watched as his eyes moved towards the ground, and he shook his head slowly from right to left.
    My mom thankfully proved him wrong though, as Christmas morning was here, and so was she! So while the unrelenting countdown still ticked loudly and steadily in our minds, we battled to stay present in the moment. She was right here, right now. This was enough. This was all we wanted for Christmas.
    We spent the day attempting to make it as normal as possible. We helped her out of bed, into a wheelchair borrowed from hospice, and into the living room to exchange gifts. Talking was now quite challenging for her, but the request to be with us all was very clear. She didn't care what condition she was in, she just

wanted to be right in the mix with everyone. Even though she could barely keep her eyes open long enough to unwrap a present or to give one, she was there. Our wish for this day came true.

    We drank eggnog, played games, and opened many gifts-a completely ridiculous number of gifts. My mom made sure to tell us a few weeks back that she wanted to have lots of gifts for everyone on Christmas Day. She had said how much she wanted to go shopping again like we usually would. She had hoped to be able to "escape" from the hospice house for a day, just to shop. My dad always cringed on hearing the word shopping, but for my mom and I, shopping was not just about stuff. It was about brainstorming gift ideas together: what would they love? What would make them feel loved? It was about knowing each other, giving the nod of approval as we tried on clothes ("yep, perfect"), or giving the look of "ummm...get it off quick and never put it back on." It was about laughing as we envisioned my dad groaning and shaking his head while we headed back to the same aisle four times, trying to decide on one little gift. It was about being together, mom and daughter.

    This Christmas, she was not well enough to go again. We knew what she hoped for though, and this was one hope we could actually help make happen. So my brothers and I decided we would each take a break from the hospice house, and run out quickly to buy ourselves gifts from mom and dad. We even wrapped them ourselves, and by Christmas morning, we had an overflowing pile of beautifully wrapped presents under the tree. We also bought gifts for the grandparents, aunts, and uncles, kids, and our spouses, all "from mom and dad," and all from just two stores. No one wanted to be gone long, so we went to the closest store possible and shopped as quickly as possible. There wasn't any time to shop around, so if it wasn't in either of those closest stores, it wasn't happening. As insignificant as gifts seemed this Christmas, we wanted any wish she had to come true. She wanted a tree full of toys and presents, and she got it. She, like us, just wanted "normal."

    Typically, Mom would be the easiest person to buy a gift for. She would love anything. She would be equally excited about a pair of socks as she would be an engraved, expensive ring. This year, however, was quite tricky. What do you buy for someone who only has a few days, if that, left? There was no gift I could give that seemed enough. I'd buy her anything. ANYTHING. There was only one gift I wished to give her though: a miracle. Instead, I was left handing her gifts I knew she would only have for a few days more. The gifts were from the heart but still seemed so trivial. Each tangible gift would then be given away or passed on to one of us soon. Let's just say this took the fun out of gift-giving.

After all the festivities, I tucked the boys into bed and we said a goodnight prayer. I only said prayers out loud to my boys, not to anyone else. Saying prayers out loud in any other situation was wildly uncomfortable for me, equally with believers and nonbelievers. So I prayed with my boys because I knew I could pray any way I wanted in front of them and they wouldn't care. I prayed for grandma and said how thankful I was that she was with us this Christmas. I prayed for them to sleep well and kissed them each goodnight.

I walked downstairs to be by her side. I assumed my typical spot by her feet and laid my hand on her leg. She had been sound asleep since this afternoon. I thought back to the morning, and how weird it felt to give her each material gift. Then I thought back to our friends from our neighborhood and church, who have been continuously asking how they could help. I told them I had no idea, just pray. Prayer, even though I didn't understand it myself, was all I could come up with. Nothing else in these moments could help at all—not a gift, not a meal, nothing. The only gift I could think of was what they were already doing: praying. Then it hit me: Gift, praying, GIFT, PRAYING. I looked at my mom. That was it! There was only one thing I could give, the only gift that could possibly make any difference to her right now: prayer. So I swallowed hard and pushed myself out of my mask that shielded me from exposing my turbulent faith. I had nothing but prayer to give. I didn't even know what I thought about it, and I definitely didn't feel comfortable doing it, especially not out loud. It was all I could give her though. It was my best shot for a gift she might actually have wanted. I took a deep breath and stepped out of my comfort zone.

"Mom," I said, waking her from a semi-sleeping state. "Hey, Mom." She blinked her eyes open and mustered a slight smile.

Okay, do it, I thought to myself. Do it quickly before you talk yourself out of it. I think this is how they say it...

"Can I pray for you, Mom?"

She responded instantly as if she knew what I was going to ask from the moment I woke her. It was like she had just been waiting patiently for me to get the words out.

"Yes, please." She looked at me like I knew what I was doing, and waited for me to begin. We had never prayed this way together before, Mom and I, or any of our family. Now here she was, saying yes, and ready to receive the only gift I could give her that might have any meaning right now. Okay, I thought, but what in the world do I pray for?

She cut off my thoughts and dove into them before I could get my first word out. Her eyes met mine again as she calmly began to lay out her list, like she had it ready and waiting for this very moment. She asked for me to pray for less or no pain when she dies. She said she was afraid of how painful the end might be. She asked me to pray for her legacy to continue through us and through generations, that she would not be forgotten. Then she asked me to pray for the most difficult thing I could imagine: that she would die soon.

I sat motionless, completely unprepared for this request. How could I possibly pray for this? She continued on seamlessly though; her mind was already made up. She said she did "not want this to be carried on for a while and interrupt our lives and be so painful for everyone." I laughed uncomfortably at this, knowing that she was completely, selflessly serious. I assured her that we would wait for years for her and be by her side every day. I told her that I wouldn't pray for her to die for us, but I would pray this for her if that was her wish. She nodded, and I held back a monsoon of tears.

The greatest gift I could give my mom this Christmas, the one she wanted more than any other, was for me to pray for her to die: to die peacefully, quickly, and for her legacy of love and selflessness to carry on.

Slowly I took her hand and began to pray. I prayed harder (if praying harder is a thing) and I prayed with more hope than ever before. I prayed with hope that this prayer stuff might actually mean something. I prayed with hope that my mom's prayers, no matter how hard they were, would be answered. This prayer was the hardest gift my mom and I ever had to find together. All the shopping and gift-giving in the world couldn't have prepared us for this last, final Christmas gift of a selfless, painful prayer.

Fraud

December 27, 2013

Then...How can we believe something we can't see? How is God so loving if someone like my mom is dying? What if this is all a fraud?

Now...Sometimes you just have to take a leap of faith.

    During my mom's last week especially, I prayed fervently for any sign of all this heaven and God stuff to be real. It didn't have to be huge, just something that showed this was not the end, and that she really was going to be okay.
    A few years prior, my husband and I had started to attend a Christian church, after leaving our Catholic upbringing many years before. We had spent many years searching other religions and beliefs to figure out what we actually believed. When we first found our new church, we were disappointed that it was Christian, but something compelled us to stay. For the first time, we had been learning and experiencing what it meant to be a true follower of Jesus. We weren't there yet ourselves, but the people we had met through our new church were the most positive, honest, kindest, judgment-free people we had ever met. We wanted what they had, and they kept pointing their lives back to Jesus.
    In these awful last few weeks though, I was thinking more and more that this was likely all just a bunch of B.S. My mom was painfully dying in front of me and everyone's prayers were completely unanswered. How could there truly be a "loving,

personal God" that our new friends talked about? Was this all just a ridiculous story people told themselves to feel better about dying?

Despite my anger and doubts, I hoped more than anything for some speck of evidence that she would really be okay. I prayed that the letter I wrote her was true, that God really was a personal God who loved her even more than I did. So I prayed. I prayed with fear, sadness, and straight-up desperation. My mom had been in a deep sleep for days and I pictured the worst. I pictured her waking up moments before she died and saying, "Kimberly, why isn't God with me? There's nothing. He does not exist. This is the end. It was all a lie."

I tried to fight this fear away the whole day, trying to hold onto some ounce of hope and gratitude in the midst of my darkest thoughts. In the evening though, the fear slowly took over as I sat by my unresponsive mom, with no answered prayers. Was this it? Is this the end and life is just one big tragic coincidence?

My brother Michael entered the room, which was a good interruption to the mental train wreck going on inside me. We hugged, and then I left to give him some time with her alone too. These moments were now clearly limited. Her door became revolving, with one entering as another one was leaving. We all ended up congregating in the hallway outside her room, wanting to give the other family members space, while also not wanting to be too far from her side.

My oldest brother Ryan was the last one to be with her and exited the room with a look of desperation. His face was filled with sorrow, his heart clearly broken. He turned toward me, and for the first time in his life, asked if I would pray. Shock, anxiety, and uncertainty instantly crept into my soul. Today I am the one thinking this is all a bad joke, and today my agnostic brother asks me to pray. This was not a simple request for him. He was stepping out of his comfort zone, toiling in the hope that there truly was more. Prayer was all that was left, even for him. In this moment, my brother had more trust in my faith than I did. While I had been thinking what a disgusting lie this all was, he had been thinking we could use some faith right now. While I was thinking screw this prayer stuff, he had been thinking now would be a good time to pray.

Not only was my faith shaking violently, but I had only

prayed out loud with anyone in my family once, with my mom just two days prior. Praying with people was so awkward to me, especially with family. He was right though, what else did we have left? I mustered up the courage and the little bit of faith I had remaining and silently begged God like a two-year-old. "Show us you are real God. Please, be real. Please show my brother he will see his mom again. Show him this is not the end." Then, I began to pray with my family out loud. On the outside, I don't remember at all how I prayed. Probably calmly, about peace, strength, etc. On the inside however, I was a complete and utter wreck. I had no idea what was actually true, and no hope that I, or any of my family, would get any answers. I had no idea that in just 24 hours, many of these answers would become crystal clear.

Words from Heaven

December 28, 2013

Then... After-life? Heaven? Angels? Nice thought, but here she is dying and I am seriously wondering if this whole thing is a really sick joke. Is she just going to die and that's it? Just gone. What if this is really it, and all this faith and hope stuff was for nothing? What if life is just one bad evolutionary coincidence where we are all strumming along in this crazy world, just waiting to turn into dust? Where are you now God, where are you?

Now... Wow! Not only is it real, it's personal. What if everyone knew how very real this all is? It truly is "the most beautiful thing."

Mom had been sound asleep for almost the entire day with the exception of maybe 20 minutes total. These waking moments were only from us desperately trying to get her attention in order to check if she needed anything. This involved us gently but firmly shaking her shoulder or leg and talking loudly, like you'd talk to a 90-year-old not wearing a hearing aid.

My family all sat by her side, watching her as she groaned now and then, moving her swollen legs restlessly as she slept. She appeared quite uncomfortable, but she was not even coherent enough to communicate a clear pain level.

"Mom? Hey, Mooooooom," we said, gently shaking her leg. She started to stir, so we tried to ask quickly before she drifted off again. "Mom, is your pain at a two or a 10?"

She struggled to even make her mouth move enough to

say the words, and then responded with a weak, almost incoherent voice, with a number of 14. We looked at each other, doubtful this was an accurate measurement. We decided to ask again for clarity, as she didn't appear to be in the extreme pain a number off the charts would describe.

"Mom, is your pain at a two or a 10?" we yelled again, as she was already asleep again in that two-second delay. Her next answer, 60 seconds after the response of "14," was "two."

We looked at each other, eyebrows raised and shoulders shrugged, unsure of what we should do next. She was unable to relay even this primal need, a need that even a newborn baby can express as soon as they leave the womb. She had been in this almost comatose state for several days now, since Christmas. After many failed attempts, we realized we needed to accept that an actual verbal response just wasn't going to happen.

Unsettled still about her possible pain, we developed a little chart that she just had to touch to communicate with us. I put my past preschool teaching skills to work and drew a green smiley face, yellow straight face, and a red sad face for pain instead of having to say a number. It seemed like this would be effective, but after just two seemingly successful attempts, even the accuracy of her pointing became questionable. Her eyes shut as she touched it, and her hand would drop quickly, as it was too weak to even point.

The hospice nurses had been by this morning and alerted us that this was the end. We could expect maybe a day, to a couple of days at the most, until her last.

Before heading to bed, the boys came in to say goodnight to grandma, as they had every night since she had come home a week ago. She was sound asleep, and I worried how disappointed they'd be when grandma didn't respond. The night before, she woke for a few seconds and her face seemed to smile slightly when she heard them come in. Even that counted as something in their book. But tonight? I doubted that she would even be able to open her eyes. I wondered how scary this must be for them, watching one of their favorite people become almost completely lifeless. They didn't care though; they wanted to see her, hug her, and be with her, even like this, just like the rest of us.

Luke, my youngest, came bouncing into the room first, dressed in the elf costume he got for Christmas. His five-year-old world seemed like the place to be, as nothing wiped that smile off his face. He was aware of what was happening, but somehow it never seemed to steal a bit of his joy. Logan followed, with an unsure smile on his face. He had this look every time he came in to see her lately—a look filled with questioning and uncertainty. He was seven, and we had been discovering that this was the hardest age for dealing with grief. He understood more than he was ready for but didn't have the words to express his feelings. He still wanted to just be a kid like Luke, but a battle had begun that pulled him back into the dark reality we were facing. Jake came in behind them willingly but cautiously, suddenly too mature for his age. He was now nine, going on 20. He had experienced more dark days in the last month than I had in my entire 31 years of life. Now he stood with the adults, also aware of the clock that ticked so loudly in our minds. My husband waited by the end of the bed, anticipating them to give her a quick goodnight kiss and be on their way. My dad remained by her side, across from me; and smiled through his heavy, bloodshot eyes at the sight of these three lively, loving boys.

    I lifted Luke onto her bed, and he laid across her to give her a big 5-year-old hug. He held it for a few seconds. I reached to help him back down off the bed and I noticed my mom's eyes starting to blink. We all watched excitedly as she then fought to open them. Yes, I thought, completely relieved. Thank you, Mom, thank you. You did it. Thank you for showing them that you know they're here. We will take it. I told the boys to look at her blinking eyes, and they all smiled a bit more naturally. It's something!

    It didn't stop there though. We watched excitedly as she took it to the next level and lifted a hand up and placed it gently on Luke's back. Gratitude filled my heart instantly, thankful for her boundless love. Luke continued his sweet grasp on her and said, "I love you, Grandma." She hugged him back, now with both arms around him. We were astonished. Then, her eyes opened wider, and she looked at him very intently. She then spoke in a clear, calm voice. A voice that we hadn't heard so strong in weeks. A voice that we thought we'd never hear again. "I love you too Luke."

    I didn't know whether to laugh or cry, so I did a little of both. I was overwhelmed with shock and filled with gratitude.

How? How can she suddenly say "I love you too Luke," when for days before, her motor control was too far gone to even drink out of a straw? Even a single number for pain was mumbled, inaccurate, and extremely weak. Now this?

She held the hug with him for several seconds and softly stroked his head. Then she turned her head toward Logan. He looked unsure but walked up close to the side of her bed and leaned across for a hug. As he hugged her, she seemed to wake even more, eyes now bright and wide.

She kept one hand on the back of his head and looked intensely into his beautiful brown eyes. Gently stroking his hair now, she began to talk—actually, fully, talk! Goosebumps began to crawl up my arms. There was clarity, peace, and strength in her voice. Her words were articulate and thoughtful. We stood completely still, awestruck as we listened. "Logan, you are so perfect, so fun, so loving to others. You have a beautiful smile and are patient and sweet.'

Shocked by what was happening, I looked around desperately for a camera to videotape this amazing moment. I looked at my dad and Paul and made a gesture for a camera. I was afraid to talk and disrupt her train of thought. They shrugged their shoulders and shook their heads no and glued their eyes back on my mom. Inside I was distraught: how could we have nothing to record this? For the first time in weeks, we had not a single moment-capturing device around. No phone, no camera, no iPad. My dad always had a camera attached to his belt (which we usually pick on him for), and now when we needed it most—NOTHING!

I tried to convince myself it was alright, that I would remember it all. I'd remember each of these loving words she was saying to him. There was no way any of us could dare to leave the room, as we feared missing or disrupting the moment, so it would have to be captured by memory only.

As she continued talking to Logan, however, I realized that I had already forgotten exactly what she said just a few sentences back. I tried to replay it in my head but I was only able to paraphrase. My translation just wasn't the same as her own, original words. Her words were intimate, and I felt the frustration again that we had nothing to capture this. I didn't want to translate; this was something extraordinary. I wanted to remember this exactly as it was.

I looked around and noticed a pad of yellow legal paper that we used to record her medications. Better than nothing, I thought, so I picked it up and began to write everything she said verbatim.

As I scribed, her words continued to flow smoothly, in a direction we never anticipated. Her words were deep, articulate, and beautiful. Her words were unlike anything I've ever heard out of her, even when she was well. Her words had strength, certainty, and wisdom to them. Her words shocked us all and sent shivers through each of us. Her words addressed things that she never talked about before, with a depth and passion like never before. Her words had experience. Her words were about God, like she somehow really knew him now, like she knew heaven.

Just a week ago, she had questioned heaven herself and had many questions that still hadn't been answered. She wanted to know if she'd still be with us, if she could see us, and told us she was scared. That conversation she had hoped to have with our pastor never happened though, because she was never alert enough again to talk about it. She had been sleeping and unable to wake for 3 days now, but it was clear...something much more had happened to her in those sleep-filled days than the rest of us knew.

Holding Logan's hand, still stroking the back of his head with her eyes directly on him, she said, "You are always so happy." Logan smiled back. She kept looking at him passionately and continued, "If you need Him, God is always with you. Love is Jesus and Jesus is God. God loves you so much. Always be so kind, so loving. You are so smart."

Then she turned back to Luke and said, "Luke, you are part of God's army. You and the beautiful elves (Logan and Luke were still dressed as elves at the time) are part of God's team. Christmas is so important. Too bad there are not more people that understand how special it is, the meaning of it. It is so special." She said a few more things about how significant Christmas is but was talking so fast I couldn't write it all.

She paused, then said to them, "God will always be with you, he will never leave you." Everyone was staring at her, mouths open. My entire body had goosebumps now.

Then she turned to Jake. His eyes stayed glued on her as he walked over. She took both of his hands in hers, lovingly and gently. Looking at him brightly, she said, "Jake, my biggest most sensitive grandson, you have so many skills, skills you don't even know you have yet. You'll always be in my heart. Grandma will always be there when you need me. Jesus will be there to keep us happy and guide us on earth."

She paused for a moment, then said, "I feel God around us right now." More goosebumps crept instantly up my already covered arms, and my hand trembled as I wrote. She said this as if He was actually present and she could physically feel him. I shivered, almost a little creeped out. Her confidence and happiness as she spoke though made me understand that whatever was happening or had happened was okay.

She continued articulately and beautifully, "Love is everywhere if you look for it. Some days you feel like you can't find it but that's okay because the next day you will see it. Sometimes the answers come right away, sometimes they don't. Even though you don't always know, everything will be okay. The answers will come eventually and I'm about to find out. Jesus will be there. It will be beautiful—beautiful, the best thing. I love you beyond love. I know you feel it. Do you feel my love? That's God. Your potential is so great; you can be anything you want to. All you boys can be anything. People are astounded by you, by your love, and by your parents."

She then looked at all of us and said, "The most beautiful family, because you bring love into the world. Keep doing what you are doing with your family and helping more and more people. Your church family is so much a part of you and starting all of this. When you eat the bread and drink the wine, it really tells us that God is your counterpart. Remember, God is you, you are God; you are all lumped together."

She then fell asleep, as our family stared at each other in awe, including the boys. They knew something was really special here, that something was very different about grandma's words. Whatever had just happened, we knew didn't come from her alone. Somehow, she knew God much more intimately now, and she was no longer uncertain about heaven. She knew where she was going, and she knew she was going soon. Just the day before, I had begged God for something like this, something showing she would be okay. Something showing he was real. I prayed at my brother's request, hoping with all my heart but doubting with all my mind that something like this could actually happen.

The language she used about her faith was unlike anything we had ever heard from her. She was passionate, articulate, bright, and full of tangible love as she spoke to each of the boys and us. My mom, who for a day or two previously and the rest of her days afterward was almost completely unresponsive, had unbelievable energy, faith, and love in these chilling yet beautiful words.

I couldn't shake the questions in my mind, and the joy in my heart for her. Somehow, in some miraculous way, while she slept, she was experiencing a glimpse of what was to come. Little did I know this night would be just the beginning of The Story that would continue to unfold.

Don't Die

December 30, 2013

Today was my brother Michael's birthday. What a birthday. I don't think I could have painted a worse picture for a birthday than this. I spent many moments by my mom's side, reminding her even while she slept, that today is a day she cannot die. Although she wasn't coherent enough to talk, I think she knew what day it was. We knew she was ready to die, since her incredible words two days prior, and the fact that the only thing she had said since was a mumbled but almost pleading statement: "I want to go." When midnight struck, I could not have been more relieved and thankful that she had made it through this day. Thanks Mom.

New Beginnings

January 1, 2014

Then… Our connections with people we love, no matter how close we are, must be lost when someone dies, right?

Now… Love has no limits. Not even death itself can sever the connection of love.

7:30 a.m.

New Year's Day. It is supposed to be a day of bright beginnings, happy memories, and looking toward the future. In past years, we have gone ice skating, sledding, baked cookies, or shared a big family dinner. Instead, I woke up to the dark, excruciating reality I was in; it's certainly not how anyone wants to spend the first day of the New Year. I wished that I could close my eyes again and wake up in a different phase of life. My thoughts went back to just a few months earlier, to our 10 unforgettable days exploring the Tetons and Yellowstone National Park. I tried to hold these memories close as I climbed out of bed, wishing we could be there together again: happy, healthy, celebrating.

I headed directly downstairs as usual and peeked quietly into her room. Phew. I took a deep breath, not even realizing I had been holding it in. She was sound asleep, but thankfully still alive. The clock ticked all too loudly. The end could come any day now, any minute.

My dad was next to her, his hand placed gently on her frail arm. He looked up at me and somberly reported she had a quiet night. Typically, this would be a positive thing. She had wished for a quiet night's sleep for the past three months. Now though, a quiet night meant her body was almost done fighting. There were a few moments when her eyes blinked open or we heard a slight moan, but she was now completely unresponsive. I noticed her breathing sounded very congested, more than any other day. I walked over to her and gave her a kiss, but there was no response this time. Typically, I would get something, but each morning's reaction this week had been progressively less. Just last week she would wake up and say good morning, give me a hug and a kiss, and ask how the boys had slept. A few days ago it regressed to just her eyes opening and a smile—a slight, but beautiful smile; a smile that I missed so much already. Yesterday her eyes opened, but on this day, there was nothing. I put her cold, limp hand in mine. I squeezed it slightly but got no response. Then I checked her pulse. Over the last few days I would periodically check it, and it had been steadily strong. I hesitantly placed my fingers on her wrist and found it after several seconds of searching. It was significantly weaker than the day before, but thankfully still steady.

  The day wore on and was unusually quiet for having four young, rambunctious kids and one newborn in the house. I wondered if they too could sense the inescapable truth: time was extremely short. Each one of us spent a lot of time in her room, in and out, just thankful for the opportunity to be sitting next to her. By the afternoon, her breathing became very heavy, and she moaned slightly here and there. We prayed that she was not in pain and continued her pain medications as scheduled just in case.

  My dad stayed next to her, continuously by her side. He had become her guardian, her advocate, and her nurse. Over the last two months, and especially in the last few weeks, he did all the unthinkable: holding a bucket as she violently vomited black bile, cleaning clothes and beds that had been soiled, giving her sponge baths in a hospital bed, and scrubbing blood off the carpet. He stared at her now, shaking his head with increasing intensity. "This can't be happening!" he cried, looking at my mom's body taken over by this evil disease. "No, this cannot be happening. Not her, not my Glenda." My brother Michael put his hand on my dad's shoulder, and tears ran steady. "It wasn't supposed to be this way. She was so healthy, so full of life. Now look at her. She doesn't deserve this." He shook his head in disbelief. "This can't be happening. Nooo!" He gasped, crying out in utter despair. His battle for understanding and anger at injustice surfaced again. "Why God, why her? She was so perfect—so incredibly perfect. Why take her?"

I sat there taking this in, wishing I had words to explain and wishing I had answers. The many questions I had been asking flooded back into my head as well. If you are as powerful as they say, God, can't you change this? Don't you love her enough to step in and change this? Why even create humans if we have to endure this pain and suffering? Why, God, why?

I looked at my dad so struck with grief and my brother lovingly by his side, longingly looking at this dying woman we each so deeply loved. My thoughts swarmed, trying to find some truth and understanding.

My own tears began as my mom's words from a few nights prior came flooding back into my head—her spirit-filled, extraordinary words that transformed my doubt into unexpected trust. The words that were not her own. For the six of us who experienced it, we knew that somehow, in some way, God was really with all of us. Those words gave us faith that she would be with God soon, and she would be eternally full of joy. Those words told us that God loves her, and that love is everywhere, even in these awful times. They gave us peace in the midst of our doubts. The words she spoke told us that no, we do not know all the answers, but to trust that God is with us, leading us to this beautiful, eternal place.

I stood by her bed wishing I had all the answers, but at the same time accepting that I wouldn't. Instead, I could only go on what I had learned and experienced on this wild journey of life so far. Seeing God speaking through her was an incredible gift, one I didn't want to lose. I thought back on her words, "The answers will come eventually and I'm about to find out. Jesus will be there. It will be beautiful—beautiful, the best thing."

I looked over at my mom, so physically frail and helpless, yet so spiritually strong. Something was special after what had happened. Her body was failing, but her faith was stronger than ever before. It was like she was rocking between heaven and earth. Was she there right now? Seeing glimpses of heaven, but coming periodically back to earth? I do not know the answers, but all I know is that something had changed in her. She was not scared anymore. The only words she had spoken in the past few days were weak and mumbled, but clear enough. "I want to go," we would hear her say every now and then. "I want to go." She was ready to go. She was excited to go.

And so, my first prayer on this New Year's Day was the most painful prayer I ever had to pray: a prayer for God to take her soon. There is nothing more difficult than praying for someone you love so much to be taken from you. However, in these last days, it was the biggest gift we could give her. She was ready, and we didn't want her to be in any more pain or suffering.

They say that hearing is the last sense to go when a person is dying, and so I leaned down and whispered in her ear, "Mom, it will be soon. Soon you will be with God, and you won't have to go through this anymore. I'm praying Mom. I know you want to go. God will take you soon."

A huge part of me didn't want these words to be true, that God would take her soon. I wanted her back desperately, but with the healthy body she once had. She didn't want to live this way, and we didn't want that for her. So with a heart that felt like it was weighed down by a ton of bricks, and tears welling up in my eyes, I prayed, "God, please take her. She wants to go and is ready. Please take her out of this awful body, please let her go to that 'most beautiful place' she talked about. God, please, please take my mom."

8:00 p.m.

"Time for bed boys," I heard my husband say.

They headed toward the stairs but stopped at grandma's room.

"Wait, we have to say goodnight to grandma," Logan replied. Jake and Luke followed, "Yea, Mom, we always say goodnight to her."

They were right, each night they have gone in to give her hugs and kisses. Tonight though, I hesitated to let them see her this way. Her eyes were now eerily open, wide and glassy. Would they only remember her in this way? The thought that this "goodnight" could be their last was too real though, and their innocent, loving hearts would adamantly refuse an answer of no. I figured it was worth the risk, so they piled in to give their grandma a goodnight hug.

Surprisingly, her eyes moved toward them as they walked into her room.

"Can she see me?" Luke asked.

"I don't know honey. I think she knows you are here though. It looks like her eyes are searching for you."

They stared at her, their expressions concerned and perplexed. They questioned why her eyes were open so wide. I questioned my decision; maybe this was not a good idea. My face probably looked as unsure as theirs.

I suggested we sing a song, to break the discomfort and lighten the mood. My mom had always loved to sing songs with the boys, and so we decided on "A Spoonful of Sugar." They sang enthusiastically, pumping their arms with the rhythm. They sang loudly, hoping their volume would bring her back, and hoping just like us for one more chance for her eyes to connect with theirs. They searched for assurance that she still was with them. Her eyes moved back and forth as they sang like she was trying to find them but just couldn't. Our show ended, and they gave her hugs and kisses, each saying "goodnight Grandma, I love you." Her only response was in her eyes, still searching but not quite finding. The boys headed out of the room, and her eyes went still.

8:30 p.m.

As my husband put the kids to bed, the rest of us stayed by her side. It had been a while since she had been changed, so we decided it needed to be done. We hated to disturb her in the state she was in, but also didn't want her to become more uncomfortable. She was moaning now and her breathing was very congested, her eyes still wide open. She had been noticeably disturbed every time we moved her on her side in the past two days. As we tried to get her attention to tell her what we had to do, she picked up one hand slightly and moved it as if she was shooing a fly away. In hindsight, she was probably trying to tell us, "don't bother," but at the time we didn't know what it meant. We were just amazed that she moved her hand at all.

I stayed by her face, as my brother and dad carefully

moved her on her side. I wrapped my arms around her, my face inches away from hers. Her eyes were still wide open and she looked painfully uncomfortable. I tried to distract her, unsure whether she was aware of my presence at all.

"Mom," I said very loudly, my eyes locked onto her glassy eyes, staring beyond me. "We're going to get you more comfortable. You'll be on your back again in a minute." Her moaning continued, and I spoke louder. "Mom, I love you. You are going to be okay. It's almost over Mom." I knew as I said this I was assuring that not only would she be on her back again in a minute, but soon she would be where she wanted to be, and all this pain would be over.

"I love you, Mom. I love you so much." I kissed her on the cheek and looked into her eyes again. "I am going to miss you so much, Mom."

Her eyes then locked on mine. She looked at me; she looked right at me. She looked clearly into my eyes. I was elated! She was still there!

Then, like the incredible person she was, she didn't end it there. Her eyes stayed locked on mine and somehow between her gargled, shallow breathing, she spoke. "I love you," she said, in a very weak but astoundingly clear voice.

My eyes overflowed with tears. I was filled with amazing love and tremendous grief at the same time. I had been so incredibly blessed to have someone who had given me a gift that some people will never know: the gift of unconditional love. Her love was so powerful that even in this state, she was able to break through this fog, through the inability to communicate, all to say these three amazing words: I love you.

9:00 p.m.

For the past two weeks, we had been relying on a booklet about dying that hospice had given us, checking the symptom timeline whenever something new came up. They described this new phase as fish-out-of-water-type breathing. It had been going on for 30 minutes now, ever since we had moved her onto her back again. The room was thick with anxiety, and my brother and I glanced at each other all too knowingly. I turned to my husband, who often becomes emotionally barren in highly emotional situations. I used to get annoyed by this, trying to shake some emotions into him. However, I knew he would tell it to me straight. I whispered in his ear as I hugged him,

"She's dying isn't she?"

"Yes, love. She is."

"Really soon?"

"Yea, I think really soon."

I checked her pulse, and it took me several minutes to find a consistent beat. It was barely there. I looked up at my brother, who had been searching on her other wrist. We shook our heads and looked back at Mom.

My eyes locked on her and the only thing I could think to do was pray. "God, please be with her right now. Please let her not be alone. God, please help her. Please just let her be happy again."

My dad was on one side of her and I was on the other, my arm around her and my face close. I whispered to her, "I love you, Mom, I love you so much. It's going to be okay soon. You will be with God soon, you will be so happy." Her eyes were now closed, and her breathing was slowing. Each of us hung on every breath, wondering if it would be her last.

My hand rested on her shoulder, and I watched as she took her final breath. Her whole body relaxed. Her fight was over. With tears falling and my heart pounding, I turned to my dad, and spoke the words I never wanted to have to say: "She's gone."

Even though we knew this was coming, shock and desperation filled the room. No matter how much time was given towards the end, it didn't take away any of the pain of her actually being gone. "No, no she's not," my dad pleaded, shaking his head. Panic set in and he held her tight. "What do we do? We have to do something! Someone call 911!" His unending desire to save her kicked in. Despite the do-not-resuscitate order we signed three weeks ago with her wishes, he wanted to try any heroic measure possible, anything for even just one more minute with her alive. My brother and I held him as he sobbed deeply, with cries of disbelief in between his attempts to rescue her. I barely squeaked out the words through my own pain, "No, Dad, she's okay now. She is where she wants to be."

I turned to my husband and hugged him tight as my tears of despair fell onto his shoulder. Excruciating sadness penetrated my soul and sounds of grief filled the whole room. I wanted to scream, to run out the door, to cry incessantly. As Paul continued to hold my shaking body, a picture of my mom hanging by the window caught my eye. She was smiling in the picture—her beautiful, happy, healthy smile. As I looked at it, an unexpected, unimaginable feeling suddenly struck me and completely took over. Just two minutes after my beloved mom had died, just seconds after feeling the most painful sadness I had ever felt, I was filled with intense, indescribable joy. Complete joy. Joy like no other.

I tried to shake it away as I wondered how I could possibly be feeling this way in such a terrible time. It felt so wrong. Maybe I was actually crazy; maybe I did officially go off the deep end. What was wrong with me that I could possibly feel such incredible joy in this moment? It took me a minute to connect the dots, but then it hit me: This was not *my* joy I was feeling. This was her joy. This was what she was feeling right now—pure, penetrating joy.

My mom and I had always been able to know what the other one was feeling, without needing to say a word. Many times I could feel her emotions, without even seeing her or hearing her reaction. It was a connection words cannot explain. It was a connection that I thought was gone forever, lost with the final beat of her heart. How could I still feel what she was feeling? How was that even possible? Questions flooded my mind, but one thing felt stronger than it ever had before: my faith. I didn't know how it all worked, but I knew she was experiencing ultimate joy that beats all else. I knew without a doubt she was experiencing heaven, "the most beautiful place" as she described it just a few days before. I knew that somehow, in some way, she was still with us. Our connection survived even the greatest odds, breaking through the barrier of life and death. I smiled through my tears that had now soaked my husband's shirt as he continued to hold me.

On this New Years Day, she entered into a new beginning that was brighter and more joyous than we could ever imagine. On this day, she really was okay. She was embarking on the ultimate beginning—the beginning of eternal joy.

The Undertaker

January 1, 2014, 10 p.m.

Then....Never even thought about an undertaker.

Now...Just like the movies!

    Forty-five minutes had gone by since she passed away. Someone had called hospice, who apparently then made all the other necessary calls. This was all new to me, never experiencing death this closely before.
    We stood in the hallway with swollen eyes and broken hearts. Her joy I had experienced only lasted for about a minute, and the mortal stabbing pain rushed back in. We had to make the excruciating phone calls to our close family, letting them know she was gone. The house was very quiet, all of us completely emotionally drained. We stood just staring at the ground, sometimes at her body, and sometimes each other, unsure of what to do next.
    Then we heard a knock on the door. Three solid, strong knocks, in perfect order. Knock... knock... knock. Oh God, I thought. It's got to be the undertaker.
    I opened up the door and was suddenly struck with another unexpected and unwanted emotion, but this time not exactly heavenly. I wanted to burst out laughing, right in the stranger's face—a laugh that would be unstoppable, uncontrollable: tears, snorting, the works.

In the doorway stood a tall, thin man, dressed in all black. He had a black cap, black gloves, black boots, and a long black trench coat. He looked like he was right out of a horror movie, picture-perfect. I couldn't believe it! I didn't know what I expected him to look like as I'm sure a guy wearing a sweatshirt and jeans would have been just as odd, but this was just too picturesque.

Then I noticed the hearse in the driveway, and it was over from there. It was all too much...

> It was pitch dark outside.
>
> It was very cold.
>
> The wind was howling.
>
> The clouds were lit up in the moonlight (seriously!)
>
> Three solid knocks.
>
> There was a tall, thin man all dressed in black.
>
> He was standing at our doorstep.
>
> A black hearse was parked behind him.

I couldn't shake his hand and escape quickly enough before I completely burst out laughing, uncontrollably. I made eye contact with nobody, as I was sure they all must be noticing the same things, and then we'd have a whole house of crazies in hysterical laughter. How could this be real? I turned away from Dr. Death and went to another room, biting my bottom lip hard in an attempt to not let any sounds come out. How crazy would it be for me to burst out laughing as the undertaker came in for my beloved mom's body?

I stayed on the opposite side of the house until I could regain control of myself. Somewhat recomposed, I walked back toward my family, while attempting to make eye contact with my brother and husband, as if to ask by telepathy, do you see how odd and hysterical this is too? But no one else seemed like they were fighting desperately to hold back their laughter. Then, I heard the wind outside howl again, and the little bit of control was now completely used up. It was just too much.

I quickly left the room and headed upstairs so the hospice lady wouldn't catch on to my craze and suggest I be taken away for mental health reasons. My husband saw my departure, but not my face. He followed me like a wonderful husband would, thinking that I was headed upstairs to break down crying again.

    The laughter started to leak through my sealed lips before I even made it into the bedroom. I made it through the door and it all broke loose. I laughed, and I laughed hard, as I tried to get him to connect the dots and see the outrageous humor. He let out some polite laughs, but it was clear he was not actually seeing it. He looked more worried than anything, likely wondering if I was losing my mind. I continued to laugh incessantly for many minutes straight. I laughed at the scene—the straight-up Hollywood production—I had just witnessed. I laughed until the scene began to close, and reality trickled back in.

When the Clock Strikes

January 6, 2014

Then...My family hadn't experienced any signs or miracles before, or I would have known about it.

Now...Apparently they have!! How had I not heard these stories before? Or, could I just not hear it then?

    A light lunch followed my mom's funeral, in the multipurpose room of the church. My grandma Dottie, my mom's mom, stopped me as I headed toward the food line to help my boys get their plates. She said she needed to talk to me as soon as I had a minute. Her tone intrigued me as she was 87 years old, and never expressed much urgency. She was wise, calm, and too sweet to ever place demands on people. I knew this must be important, whatever it was. I told her I'd be right back and made guesses in my head as I loaded the boys' plates with more food and treats than they could possibly eat. Maybe she found something of my mom's she wants to give to me? Maybe she had something for the boys—maybe a gift, maybe a picture?

    I sat the boys down with their food and walked quickly back to my grandma. She smiled and turned toward me as she saw me coming. I knelt beside her and she began to tell the story. Tears began to overwhelm her eyes.

    "Have you heard the story about the grandfather clock, the one in my kitchen?" she asked, smiling.

    "No, I don't think so," I said, wondering what this has to do with today.

"Well, it's very old. It was your great, great grandfather's clock. The kind you have to put oil in. Before your grandfather died, 35 years ago, the clock had been broken for years. We never had time to fix it, nor did we know who to take it to since they didn't make them anymore. So it stayed on our wall as a decoration—broken. The day your grandfather was buried, we came home after the funeral and sat down at the kitchen table. We heard a ticking sound and Kimberly..." She stopped for a couple of seconds, shaking her head. She looked up at me and said, "I don't know how this could have happened, but that grandfather clock started working. It had been broken for so long." Her head was still shaking back and forth in disbelief, like it was the day it happened.

"Wow," I said, "I never heard that story before."

She looked away for a minute and used a tissue to catch her tears. "Yes," she continued, "we never understood it, but we knew it was him somehow. We couldn't explain it; we just knew it."

I could see a look of both pain and wonder covering her face. Holding back her tears, she continued, "Do you remember the other clock in our kitchen? The one with the pictures of the birds that makes the different bird sounds for each hour?"

"Yes," I said, nodding my head, and wondering where this was going, "I remember that one."

"Well, it has been broken for years too. Your mom would notice every time she came to visit that it was still not working. It did keep the time, but when each hour struck, the wrong bird noise would sound: the cardinal would whoo, the owl would chirp. They were all off. A single bird hasn't been right in years."

I chuckled and added, "Yea, I remember that clock. The boys pointed it out the last time we visited and thought it was pretty funny."

"Well," she said, "Yesterday, before we had to leave for the viewing for Glenda, we sat down to eat lunch in the kitchen. It happened to be about noon, and noon was supposed to be the owl sound on the clock, the chirp that we had heard for years from that owl. As George and I sat there quietly eating, the hour hand struck." She shook her head as tears began gliding down her cheeks. "Would you believe it? The owl whooed, Kimberly. It whooed! It was right!"

My tears began to fall, as goosebumps crawled up my arms. My grandma looked at me with complete awe entangled with the deep sadness that had covered us all in the past few days. "Now how could that happen? There's just no other way it could be." She shook her head and looked at me, "It was Glenda, Kimberly. I know it. It was my Glenda."

When I got home from the funeral, I opened up my journal and began to write my grandma's story down, not wanting to forget any part of it. I looked through the previous few pages at things I had jotted down in the chaos and pain of the last few weeks. I took out the folded yellow paper I had scribbled frantically on while my mom was talking unusually about God just a week before. I looked at my list of things I was thankful for, something a friend had recommended I try to do during this time. With all of the emotions I was feeling that day, just hours after my mom's funeral, the one emotional response I didn't expect was curiosity. I couldn't help but wonder what God was doing here, and why it seemed like something beautiful was unfolding amidst the darkest days of my life. A story seemed like it was being read to me in real-time, and the type of story I never believed was possible.

Dinnertime in Pennsylvania

January 8, 2014

Then...Death is the end of tangible connections, even with loved ones. We have old memories, but no new memories to be made.

Now...Wow. Just wow! How can this be possible? Coincidence? No way. Coincidences don't give you instant goosebumps. Coincidences have some sort of explanation.

Now two days after her funeral, my husband Paul, our boys, and I loaded into our minivan for the trip back to Pennsylvania. It was a hard ride home, filled with lots of tears off and on. We had all been in New York for the last month, but the thought of now driving home was so final.

My husband and I talked about weird things we wished we didn't have to, like what kind of vessel we should use for my mom's ashes. Our family had decided on cremation, so my brothers and I needed to find something small for each of us to keep a tiny portion of our mom's remains. I was quite unsettled about the whole ashes thing and found it quite odd. Now, we were driving along asking questions like: what in the world do we put them in? What could I possibly find that would be special enough for her ashes?

An hour or two from home, a little box came to mind that my mom had given me years ago. It was very pretty, but I never used it because I thought it resembled a mini casket. Being sometimes too honest, I told her this shortly after she gave it to me. Thankfully, she and I often thought similarly, so she laughed and agreed. It was made out of stone, the top engraved with a woman holding a flower. The more I thought about it, the more I realized it would be perfect for her ashes. It was small, pretty, and from her…just right, assuming I still had it, that is. It had been years since I had even opened it, and I couldn't remember the last time I saw it.

Pulling into our driveway, the finality of her death suddenly became real. I fought back tears as I thought about the fact that my mom would never again be coming to our house. She would no longer be opening her passenger door as the boys nearly tackled her with hugs. She would no longer be smiling at me as she walked up to our porch, ready with some compliment that instantly made me feel treasured.

As I opened the front door, I felt as if I had just arrived home from a different world. A world I never wanted to be a part of, but a world that now seemed more normal than my quiet, foreign home. The trauma that my family and I had just gone through in the last month suddenly became real. Even though the boys and Paul were there buzzing around, talking, and unpacking, I felt completely alone.

I stood in our doorway for a few seconds fighting back tears, then remembered something that felt more normal than this house right now: finding the box for the ashes. Just hours ago it was a weird thought, but now it was the only thing that felt right. Instead of unpacking or starting dinner for our hungry kids, I headed directly upstairs to my room on a mission.

I found the box quickly. It was sitting on our bathroom shelf, covered in a nice layer of dust. "Perfect," I thought as I grabbed it, relieved it was still around. I opened it to check what I would need to dump out to make room for her ashes.

Instant tears came to my eyes. I fell to the ground as I held the open box in disbelief, now crying while simultaneously laughing uncontrollably. There, in this box that hadn't been opened in over a decade, were 12 missing earrings of mine from throughout the past 15 years or more. Some were earrings that I had saved the match for years, but eventually gave up searching and threw the lone one out. Some were matches to lone earrings I still had. Some, I didn't even remember.

Her words from that odd conversation a week before she

died came flooding back to my mind. The conversation that I had since forgotten about, the one that I filed away and labeled "likely never going to need to remember this again," was now so apparent. Her words were clear and confident. "Every time you lose an earring, remember that I love you, and know that I am with you." I stared at the earrings in front of me as I sat on the bathroom floor, both laughing and crying. I felt hope begin to displace the pain and loneliness that had been there just moments before. I felt hope that maybe somehow, however this crazy stuff works, she really was still with us. I felt hope that somehow, in this new scary world without my mom to reach out to me, I was not alone.

Dinnertime in Lockport, NY
January 8, 2014

Before...Maybe people just overthink things that happen and then it seems more like a sign or miracle.

Now...What if the person is too upset to even think though? What if they are not even looking for it?

He sat down at the dining room table in a now completely quiet house. The house had been stirring for the past two months with people in and out like bees. Family, friends, co-workers, and nurses were constantly in and out to help or visit my mom, comfort my dad, run errands, cook meals, etc. The funeral had been over for a couple of days now though, and it had been time for everyone to go back to their normal lives—everyone but him.

Instead, he sat at the kitchen table in the most abnormal way possible for him, alone. My mom was an amazing cook, making everything from scratch and often grown in her own garden. Everything she made always tasted delicious. The kitchen had always been an eventful, joyous place. Now it was a place of sorrow and emptiness.

My dad sat in front of the meal he had microwaved, and the grief overtook him. He was now on his own. There would be no more homemade meals with his wife of 38 years. How could he possibly even go on without her by his side? Tears dripped, as they had regularly each day now. He mustered up the strength to attempt the first bite of this meal he never wanted, and that's when he heard it: the silent house became filled with the soft, enchanting cello music my brother had recorded for my mom to comfort her when she was sick.

He sat there in awe, but even more in disbelief. Where was this music coming from? Why was it suddenly playing at this moment? How did it even start playing? Despite his passionate prayers for a sign that she was okay, he did everything he could to rationalize this "coincidence." He got up from the table slowly, almost a little frightened, and walked over to the CD player. He figured it must somehow be on a timer. After thorough inspection though and not finding a timer or any other logical explanation, he called my brothers and I. He assumed we must be able to explain this "coincidence," doubting that any of what he prayed for fervently was actually possible. He was in too much pain to process this, and almost preferred it to have a clear, sensical answer at this point.

None of us had any answers though. The only thing we had were chills, chills from hundreds of miles away just hearing about what had happened. A CD player playing the music made especially for her, at the time of his first bite of a meal alone. This was too insane to be a coincidence, too perfectly orchestrated. After he told me about the music, I shared with him what happened to me that evening with the earrings. We cried together on the phone, with many moments in silence, just in awe of how this could be. Despite what my mom had said to me before she died, despite his desperate prayers for a sign that she was somehow still with us, despite all we hoped for, it was obvious that none of us had ever actually believed what we were hoping for could really happen.

The radio did not turn on again the next day, or any day beyond that, with the exception of my dad intentionally turning it on. There was no answer, no answer short of a miracle.

Grocery Shopping

January 10, 2014

Then...I had no idea how it felt to have just lost a loved one.

Now...Your world is completely flipped upside down, and the things that continue as usual feel very out of order.

I walked into our local grocery store, covered with grief from head to toe. I was completely amazed. Everybody was just carrying on like nothing had happened—NOTHING. They passed by me, completely unaware that my mom had died just nine days before. How do they not know? How could they not see this grief coating me? How could they just go on as normal? How could things still possibly be the same as a month ago?

Strangers walked by, focused on their shopping. I wanted to scream. I wanted to scream loudly. *MY MOM JUST DIED! I AM DYING INSIDE! HOW CAN YOU JUST KEEP GOING?* I wanted to wear a flashing sign that let people know. I wanted to let people in on the pain that had been suffocating me, to let them be part of this world I was now in because I felt completely lost and alone in their world. I somehow made it to the register with less than half of what I went there for.

The cashier went on with her job as if nothing had happened. She said simply, "Hello. How are you?" I hesitated and tried to calm all the screaming that had been silently happening for the last 10 minutes. She was expecting only one answer. The answer we all give. I pulled myself together and temporarily entered this strange world. Then I said the one and only word I spoke the whole shopping trip, the word that was as far from the truth as possible, but the word I was supposed to say: "Good."

Shoes

January 15, 2014

Then...Grief seems so extremely painful. I want nothing to do with it.

Now...Grief is so extremely painful. It makes you realize everything you had, and everything you lost. You begin to suddenly cherish little things that before went unnoticed.

    I opened the door to my parent's house, the house my mom picked for large, fun family gatherings and making memories with the grandchildren, for lots of big, home-cooked meals. Now, it was a place of mourning. As much as she put into this house to make it a beautiful, welcoming home, her absence made it feel like a consuming dark hole.
    I walked by the curtains and pillows we picked out together and headed upstairs where her coats, clothing, and shoes had been laid out. We needed to go through what to keep, if anything, and what to give away. I spotted a well-used pair of Crocs that she had worn for several summers. They were beige with lots of dark mud stains; only memory could tell they were once white. I could barely look at them, at these shoes that she would never again wear. I thought of all the memorable times, from the beach to her garden, where these shoes were worn. I considered keeping them, these dirty old shoes, and was certain I would wear them if they weren't two sizes too big. I considered what I should do with them, as throwing them out was not an option. I could just put them in a box somewhere. Nah, I thought,

then I wouldn't even see them. I thought I could put them on our shoe shelf, even though they would never be worn. Then I realized that would be weird. My heart physically hurt as I deliberated over what to do with this pair of shoes that once carried a life so full of love and joy. The only thing I wanted was for my mom to be alive, walking around in these Crocs. I looked at them and felt completely empty—as empty as the pair of shoes.

The Man by the Casket

Mid January 2014

Then...Connections out of this world? Seeing spirits? Sensing presence? Sounds like a late-night TV hoax. No way, not in this world.

Now...Umm, what? Very, very strange. But, if God is real and God really is all we say he is, then why not? If we believe God is actually real, we cannot put limits on him. Believing in who God fully is would mean angels are real, the holy spirit is real, miracles are real, and even the utmost impossibility would be possible.

    Just a couple of weeks after my mom's funeral, my dad called and shared a very unusual conversation he had with a friend. He was a down-to-earth professional whose job was to focus on the facts. He was well-respected both at work and in the community. My dad went to meet with him about work but unexpectedly came out with a lot more than that.
    For this book, I will use the name Josh when talking about my dad's friend, as this is not something Josh ever shared publicly. Josh had attended my mom's funeral and knew that my dad was having a hard time since she passed away. When they started to talk though, he could see that my dad was not doing well at all. He gave my dad a big hug and expressed his condolences. He looked at my dad for a few extra seconds and then asked my dad if he could share something with him that may help a little, even though he wouldn't usually share this sort of information. My dad could tell Josh was not very comfortable sharing whatever it was but had

a feeling by his demeanor that something big was coming.

Josh went on to explain that he has had a gift since he was a little kid, in which he experiences things outside what most humans would consider possible. He sees images and smells aromas that others do not, and can sense the presence of people who have died. He began to share many examples of experiences with people in his family after they passed away and the different ways he has seen or experienced already deceased family members around them at their death. My dad sat still as he was talking, completely in awe of what this seemingly "normal" man was telling him. He also sat with chills, having a feeling there was a bigger, more personal reason for Josh's openness with him.

Josh then asked my dad if roses and gardenias meant anything to him. My dad said he couldn't think of anything specifically but knew my mom liked all kinds of flowers. My dad said he would ask my grandma, who knew more specifics about my mom and flowers. Josh then went on to describe his experience at my mom's funeral. He said when he arrived, he picked an empty pew to sit in near the back. When he sat down, he instantly had an odd feeling that he needed to move over, like he was sitting very close to someone. He instinctively scooted right over to make room. As he was sitting there alone, he began to smell a strong aroma of roses on one side of him and gardenias on the other. There was no one that he could see sitting anywhere close to him, but there were clearly two distinct aromas. In his experiences, this was not the first time he had sensed a very strong, aromatic smell present at a funeral that others did not smell at all. Every time he had experienced this, the fragrances he smelled were associated with the person who died or their loved ones who have died before them. My dad sat completely bewildered, in awe of what Josh was exposing about himself and the fact that this event somehow included my mom, at her funeral.

Josh paused briefly, making sure he hadn't totally lost my dad to thinking he was completely insane. Seeing my dad was still with him, he continued. He said that toward the end of the service, he went up for communion with everyone else. The song "I Can Only Imagine" was playing. As he walked toward the front of the church, Josh told my dad that he saw a man, tall with red hair, cut short, and blue eyes standing behind my mom's casket. He said this man had one hand gently resting on top of it. The man was smiling a "toothy" smile. Josh said the man turned toward him, looked right at him, and smiled.

My dad sat glued to his seat, wondering what this all meant. Josh asked him if he knows anyone who fits this description. My dad thought for a minute and could not think of anyone, but told Josh that without a doubt, no one was behind her casket during communion. Josh shook his head, and said "No. Who do you know who has already passed away and looks like this?" It then hit my dad immediately: he was describing my mom's dad to the T. Her dad had died 35 years prior, and was tall, with blue eyes, short red hair, and a toothy smile. The connection sent chills throughout my dad's body. He sat there across from Josh, shaking his head in disbelief, but also somehow believing at the same time. Even just weeks ago, he never would have thought any of this was possible at all. Now, how could he not? Josh had no reason to share this with him, and he put himself at risk by doing so. My dad could have called him insane, could have mocked him, could have exposed his secret to others. It was not something Josh shared or wanted people to know, as he knew how the world would perceive this unusual gift. Yet he put his reputation on the line for the chance that it might help my dad.

When my dad called and told me this story, we put our heads together to find the loophole. How did Josh know what my grandfather looked like? He barely knew my mom and certainly did not know any of her family. There were no pictures of her dad he could have seen, and we didn't even have any pictures of him that matched Josh's description. In the two pictures we did have stored away in an old photo album, he was older, the pictures were black and white, and he was not smiling. How Josh could have known what my grandfather, who hadn't been alive for decades, looked like was unexplainable.

My dad then asked my grandma about the roses and gardenias. She knew the roses right away. Her mom had planted roses along the edge of the creek bank where they used to camp when Glenda was growing up. My mom used to love going there and was always excited about the roses blooming. The red roses still flourish along the creek today. The gardenias were a little more of a head-scratcher. She knew my mom liked gardenias but could not place them exactly, though their significance would eventually make its way into The Story again.

If we hadn't experienced some of our own unexplainable events already, I would have laughed at this man's story. However, if I had experienced my mom saying spiritual things on her deathbed that were not her words, and signs like earrings, clocks, and music, how is it that different from what Josh experienced? Maybe sometimes, the fact that something is unexplainable actually makes more sense than trying to explain it? Maybe we cannot box up every answer in a nice package when talking about things that are beyond our human understanding, like angels, miracles, and even God? Maybe unexplainable is just what it is. Maybe unexplainable is actually more reasonable.

More Earrings

January 23, 2014

Then...How do I do this life without my mom?

After...How can she still possibly show up right at the perfect time, even after she has died? Incredible!

By late January, life was returning to normal, which wasn't an easy thing. My youngest, Luke, had started kindergarten in the fall and I had anticipated being a mess as I adjusted from having a child home with me every day for the last eight years, to no one. The first few months of the empty nest were taken up by my mom's battle, so in many ways, it was actually a gift that the boys were all in school.

Now, as a new normal crept in, I began to fully feel the pain of all the change and loss. I had such a clear role as a stay-at-home mom/ working part-time, and then as a caretaker and cheerleader for my mom. As the dust began to settle, it all began to hit me. Who am I? What am I supposed to do now? What's my purpose?

After many nights of my husband patiently listening as I repeatedly asked the same questions, I still didn't have any clear answers. I wanted someone to tell me, "Kim, do x, y, and z. This will be the ticket to a beautiful self-identity and happy future." But since that didn't happen, I continued to dwell on the topic. The hardest part was there were many options for what I could do, but what I really wanted to do was the craziest choice I could imagine—something I never planned for, but that I was feeling "called" to do: write.

The idea of writing regularly, especially to write a book, was like saying that I wanted to become a pro surfer or professional clown. I have never surfed in my life, and juggling…forget it. Give me one ball, no problem, but two and it's all over! The idea of being "called" to do something felt even crazier. Although I clearly felt it, I was still highly skeptical of that word: called. Can God really "call" us to do something? But every way I turned, I was pointed in the same direction…write. I fought hard to ignore this.

One morning, I drove to a park to do some trail running and to clear my mind. In the last couple of weeks, my mind had been completely consumed over my lost identity. I thought about it continuously as I ran though, and by the end, I was more tired from thinking than from running.

As I pulled back into the driveway, sweaty and frustrated, I realized how much I wished my mom could help me sort all this out. I needed to bounce all this off of her. I needed her to be here to listen like she always did. I needed her to help guide me. She knew me well, and I needed someone to take the wheel from me and tell me what direction to drive. I continued to sit in the car and became increasingly mad. Then I became furious.

"Mom, I need you!" I screamed. "I am so lost mom, I have no idea what to do." Tears poured incessantly down and my shirt became more drenched in tears than sweat. "I miss you mom, I miss you so much! Where are you? Where are you, mom?"

My mind switched back to writing, which turned me suddenly into a 13-year-old, complete with attitude and disgust. "Mom, I CANNOT write, that's crazy. Why do I have this story? What am I supposed to do with it? I can't do this. I really need you. Where are you?"

I continued to yell and sob in the driver's seat of our van for several minutes. I desperately wanted clarity. I never had felt so lost in my entire life as I did at this moment. Then, through clouded vision, a little box caught the corner of my eye. I knew what was in there, and the very thought of it made my heart start to race even harder.

It was a box of my mom's earrings that I had brought to the funeral home, to see which ones would go best with the outfit we picked out for the viewing. I had brought five pairs and left the chosen earrings with the mortician. The other pairs I put safely back in the box, brought to my van, placed in the center console, and hadn't touched them since. The box had sat in the same spot for the past three weeks... top tightly on with no one quite sure what to do with it.

As I sat there crying, I picked up the box for the first time. Tears poured as I continued my rant of how much I needed her. I opened the box, expecting to see the four pairs of earrings I had put there a few weeks prior. Instead, sitting in the box were two lone earrings, both missing their match. I looked around our recently cleaned-out car, and the other earrings were nowhere to be found. In fact, I have never found them, even years later.

Instantly, my body was covered with goosebumps. Then, much like the time when I found the earrings in the vessel for her ashes, I burst out laughing in amazement. How could this sign, paired with the words she attached to this sign, be any more perfect for this moment? "Whenever you lose an earring, know that I am with you. Remember how much I love you. Think about what is going on in your life and what I am trying to tell you."

I laughed, cried, and my brain relaxed for the first time in weeks. Then I smiled, walked inside, and started to write.

Pictures

March 7, 2014

Then...Some things only happen in the movies.

Now...Apparently my life is a movie.

      I had been looking through pictures to make a scrapbook of my mom for my boys. I asked to borrow my dad's camera to look through his photos as well. There were pictures from our trip to Yellowstone, some pictures in the pool at their new house, and then pictures that seemed like a good idea at the time to take but were hard to look at now.
      As I sifted through the pictures from when she was sick, one instantly caught my eye. I did a second take, not believing what I was seeing. In front of me were not one but two photos that could not have been, pictures that instantly raised every hair on my arms, and honestly... completely weirded me out! I almost dropped the camera as I stared in disbelief at these impossible photos.
      Right in front of me were photos taken on that fateful night just a few days before she died; the night when my mom shared about God in such an unbelievable way. No one in that room had a camera and no one left to get one, as we each became statues as soon as she began to speak. I had asked everyone for a camera as we stood around her bed, desperately wanting to record what she was saying, but no one had one. It just didn't make sense. How could it be?
      I continued scrolling through and found several more

photos. I was excited but also still creeped out. There, clear as day, were pictures taken from not just one side of her bed, but both sides, capturing her as she lovingly talked to the kids. There were even some with me in the background, furiously writing on that yellow notepad. I looked through them many times as I laughed and cried. I could not make any sense of it, despite my efforts. By this time, I was beginning to realize that no matter how hard I tried, there was much that was outside of my capacity to understand.

Across Faith

March 2014

Then... Why would these signs only be happening to certain people of a certain faith? God is bigger than that, right?

Now....No exclusions apply.

My brothers, Michael and Ryan, live in North Carolina. Michael and his wife, Alesha have two awesome kids, and Ryan and his wife, Melissa, have a spunky, fluffy fur baby. While there is so much we think similarly on, one of the topics in which we do not fully align is our faith. While they are all open to the idea that there may be something bigger in this universe than us, they would not have called themselves Christians or believers of any specific religion. They do not have spiritual practice as a regular part of their lives. Following the first few months after our mom passed away, most of our family had dreams about her, but only my dad, my grandma, and I had the crazy things happen while awake. I didn't understand why and hoped more of our family, no matter what they believed, would have their own incredible experience. Then the unexplainable happened, again and again, to more than just the few of us.

Michael...
My brother Michael woke up one morning at his house, with Alesha still sound asleep next to him. He decided to walk downstairs quietly to check on his little ones. Jack, who was five

months old at the time, and Zinnea who was three, were also still sound asleep.

He walked across the house toward the kitchen when he heard a simple "Good morning," clear as day, like someone was in his living room. He turned around but no one was there. He looked outside to see if maybe it was a neighbor, but no one was around. Then he heard it again very clearly, one more time, "Good morning," and this time he instantly stopped his searching. He recognized the voice and knew unmistakably who it was, though he had no idea how it could be. Just like she was right there in the room with him, my mom had said, "Good morning."

When Alesha woke up, he explained what happened. He went back to logic mode, figuring there must be some other explanation. He asked Alesha if there were any toys in the house that played the greeting, trying to find a solution to this puzzle. There were no talking toys. He then asked Alesha to go outside and yell good morning, thinking maybe a neighbor's loud greeting had carried into their house. When she yelled from outside though, from several different locations, he did not hear a single sound.

After all logical explanations were ruled out, Michael came to the conclusion that his gut had first told him: the cheerful greeting was somehow, in some miraculous way, from our mom.

Ryan...

My brother Ryan had a similar experience. He was working from home one day, alone in his house. He was walking through his living room when he heard someone say, out of nowhere, "You are on my mind every day." It sounded like someone was right behind him, like the person was in his house. He looked around to see who said it, assuming someone must have come in, but no one was around. He then looked outside as well but didn't see anyone.

Not finding any other answers, he paused his search and replayed the voice in his head, "You are on my mind every day." He realized that he knew that voice very well and that there actually was no explanation. He got the instant goosebumps many of us had experienced over the last few months. It was the voice of our mom.

Alesha...

My sister-in-law, Alesha, was in a very stressful time of her life. She had just had a baby three months prior, and just a couple of weeks following baby Jack's arrival into this world, my mom's health took the sudden turn for the worst. She was an amazing wife, making the long trip from North Carolina to New York with an infant, and staying by our family's side for weeks without hesitation. After the funeral, life had begun to return to normal and the stress from the previous couple months was stacking up. Despite all of this, following the loss of my mom, Alesha felt inspired to rise beyond the stressors of daily life and be the best wife she could possibly be to my brother. She decided to write him a letter, explaining the challenge she was giving herself to be the best wife and mom that she could be.

The day after she gave the letter to my brother, a text message from an unknown number was sent to her that made her instantly stop. As soon as she read it, she immediately thought of my mom. The text read, "How much is the best you can do?" She texted the number back, but they had no idea what she was talking about. They said they had not texted her anything—not on purpose and not by mistake. Alesha knew they were telling the truth; it would have been too big of a stretch to be a coincidence. How could someone have randomly, accidentally texted her a question that was so fitting to a sentiment she had only shared with my brother the night before? She knew this message was from my mom, confirming her letter, and challenging her to be an even better wife and mom than she could imagine.

Sewing Memories
April 4, 2014

Then...Love between a parent and child is such a special bond.

Now...Love between a parent and child is such a special, eternal bond.

    I had learned at the funeral for the first time that my grandma was a believer of signs and miracles since she had experienced unexplained phenomena around my grandfather's and then my mom's passing. She had learned to doubt a little bit less than the rest of us and take it for the miracle that it was. That said, she still found it incredible when something miraculous happened. She had already told me the story of the clock, but another story came a few months later.

    My grandma was sitting at her sewing machine one day making something for my cousin. As she sat there, she was reminded of my mom and how they spent hours sewing together, making Raggedy Ann dolls when she was young. Just a few months ago, they had sewed stuffed animals for my brother's children. She sat trying to concentrate on the item she was sewing instead of the sadness inside. Her youngest child was gone, "My Glenda," as she had always lovingly called her.

    As she began to sew again, she felt a firm hand on her shoulder, like someone was greeting her or trying to get her attention. She turned around, but no one was there. She called for her husband (she had remarried some years after my mom's father had died of cancer), and he replied from another room. She walked into the living room where he was watching TV and asked if anyone else was in the house, but it was just them. It didn't make sense, no logical explanation was working out. She looked around some more, and then the realization hit her...My Glenda!

Of course, it was her, she thought to herself. As illogical as it seemed, she knew it had to be. There was no other answer than her daughter showing her love with a simple, sweet touch. Her doubts withered, and she instead soaked in the joy of the experience. Her Glenda was still there at the sewing machine, showing her love at just the right moment.

Coins

April 2014

Then...My mom loves her grandchildren like crazy.

Now...Yep! She sure does.

      Luke hadn't received a sign from my mom yet like some of the rest of us had. I hadn't thought of the boys needing a personal sign for each of them, but I guess it made sense for a child to want or even need that. They compartmentalize a lot. Things are very clearly theirs or not theirs when they are young, and apparently, this was one of those things.
      Luke approached me one day, looking very sad, and expressed his wish for a sign from Grandma. "I wish she would help me find coins," he said. It seemed random to me, but not to a six-year-old. But at this point, after all that had happened, I figured why not. I told him to go ahead and pray or ask grandma (still not sure what the procedure is here) and let it be known that he would like her to help him find coins someday. I watched him walk away, in awe by how bold and trusting a six-year-old can be. He knew clearly what he hoped for and wasn't afraid to ask.
      I'm not sure exactly what he did after this conversation, but for the next couple of weeks straight, Luke found coins every single day. He found coins in the house, in his room, in every store we went to, on sidewalks, etc. They would be right in front of him as he was walking or standing in line at a checkout. Other family or friends could be searching an area and see nothing, and then

Luke would come over and find a coin. It got to the point where it was almost a little obnoxious how many coins he found. With each one he found though, he would hold it up with the biggest grin on his face. You could feel the excitement pouring out of him. His grandma, one of his most favorite people, was still showing him how very loved he was.

A Touch from Heaven
July 2014

Then...Connections between earth and heaven would be kind of creepy.

Now...Yes. kind of creepy, but a kind of creepy that you don't want to go away.

   I stirred in my bed, half awake, half asleep. What's this smell? The intensity of it increased, waking me up more. I tried to shake it off so I could keep sleeping, but the potency only intensified. I thought maybe a container of soap or a bottle of perfume had spilled. I tried to ignore it so I could drift away again. The smell became so extreme, however, that I began to taste it. It was as if a dozen extremely fragrant flowers were being held right up to my nose, maybe even in my nose. It penetrated all my nasal passages and then began to seep into my taste buds. I had no choice but to fully wake up now and track down where this smell was coming from. I glanced at the clock: 3:31 a.m. I looked over to my husband...sound asleep. I looked at the windows... completely shut. Even if they were open, only a tanker truck filled with rose perfume spilling hundreds of gallons right on our front yard could create this aroma.

  By this point, the fragrance was so overwhelming that I was almost gagging. It is one thing to smell a beautiful scent and another thing to taste it! I looked at our bedroom door, which, as usual, was slightly ajar so we could hear the boys. They were still asleep in their rooms. I attempted to wake up Paul to see if he could help figure this out, but he just groaned and turned away. I laid back down, defeated in my search for an explanation. The smell, however, was incessant, and connections began to fire in my mind.

Flowers: my dad's friend Josh and the smell of gardenias and roses at the funeral.

Roses...all along the creek bank where my mom's family liked to camp.

Flowers...planted along our pathways.

It struck me that there may be one explanation, one that was seemingly impossible and just plain crazy. As I laid there though, I thought of the other unexplainable things that had already happened, things I would have never believed before she passed. As my mind cleared, only one answer seemed possible...Mom, is that you? Could it be? A smile spread across my face, as I stopped trying to rationalize and just enjoyed it. The smell continued for maybe another minute, and then in a split second, completely disappeared.

Questions came back: Was she just here? How could it be? I thought of how strangely incredible this was, and how unexplainable. Could it actually be her? Maybe I am just crazy? I turned to my side, accepting that there was no clear answer, and tried to fall back asleep.

But then it got crazier...

It started on my hands, and then it slowly moved up my arm, and then to my shoulder. It felt like a light touch and caused the hairs on my arms to tickle like crazy. I froze, trying not to freak out. What in the world is happening? I then felt the sensation around my face, moving up my cheekbone to my forehead. It moved to my back, making me want to scratch it, but I didn't dare move. Although whatever was happening was really strange, I did not want it to end. The problem-solver part of my brain kicked in again. A fan, a window? I remembered I already checked the window, and there was no fan on me. And the touch was too isolated to be a general thing like a breeze. The flowers first, followed by this? Nothing logical worked.

The touch moved back and forth on my arm like a mother so gently caressing her child. Joyful tears filled my eyes, and I smiled as I laid still and soaked it in. The sensation continued for about a minute, and the need to itch my back became overwhelming. Finally, I couldn't take it anymore. I broke down and itched it quickly, hoping it wouldn't make the whole thing stop. I laid calm and still again, and the touch continued now only on my arms and face as if she understood touching my back was making me tickle uncomfortably. It was such a slight sensation as if you were moving your hand up and down your arm, just barely touching your hair.

After about 60 seconds, just like the flower smell, it stopped suddenly and completely. I laid there, as peaceful as ever. No more questions swarmed my brain. I smiled, joyfully overwhelmed by her presence, and said softly, "Hi mom."

For months, I searched for a gardenia at different nurseries to see if that was what I smelled. I had never smelled a gardenia before, but I knew the smell was not quite roses. Sure enough, when I finally found one, the fragrance was unmistakable- it was gardenia that filled the air that night. It was the missing link to the aroma my dad's friend, Josh, had experienced at the funeral. I sniffed the gardenia repeatedly as I stood in the middle of the store, smiling ear to ear.

Coming Through

August 1, 2014

Then… One of the most important people in my child's life has been ripped away from them.

Now… Love finds a way through even the most impossible obstacles.

Something wasn't right. My laid-back, fun-loving boy had been one huge mess of emotions—one moment hysterically laughing, the next in full tears. I had tried to pry it out of him, trying to find out what was going on in every way I could, but he wouldn't open up. Being only eight, I realized it was likely he couldn't pinpoint it himself, let alone explain it to me.

As I was cleaning up from dinner, Logan hesitantly walked over to me. I could tell by his approach something was up. "Mom," he barely squeaked out before the tears started to form. His eyes began to fill with tears and his voice was shaky. This looked big. I stopped what I was doing and got down on my knees to hug him at his level. He immediately fell into my arms and began sobbing uncontrollably. The pressure I had seen building up over the last couple of days reached its capacity, and the geyser let loose. "I just want her back, Mom. I want her back, I want her back," he cried repeatedly.

Half of me was ecstatic—finally, kid, finally! The other half of me held the stabbing pain in my heart that I felt for him. Although it was awful to watch him grieve, I had been waiting for this moment for many months now. She was so close to the three boys. They shared the most beautiful grandma-grandchild bond, and she played such a huge role in their lives since before they were even born. Logan had broken down only twice before, once at a bowling alley two weeks before she passed and once at the funeral. Since then, he had closed up like a clam, only answering with a couple of simple words each time I tried to pry open his shell. This evening though, he was opening up himself, unable to contain the hurt and the questions any longer.

 I held him tight as he continued to sob for the next five minutes, with no audible words. I repeated "I'm sorry, I'm so sorry," over and over. He then took a deep breath and said, "It's no fun without grandma here. I want her *here*." I heard the anger in his voice, expressing how it's just so wrong and so unfair. I tried to console him as he shook in my arms. "I know buddy, me too. She's still with us though." He began to cry harder, and said in a heartbroken voice, "Mommy, why haven't I gotten a sign from her? I haven't even had a dream. I want one mom. I want a sign." And at this, the sobs increased in intensity. My heart was officially in pieces. Not only was he missing her so badly, he felt unchosen and forgotten. Many people had a sign or a dream at this point, including both of his brothers. Luke now had the coins, Jake had a beautiful dream, but Logan had nothing.

 There were now two exploding geysers in the room. All I could get out was, "I know, buddy, I know." I tried desperately to take deep, quiet breaths, as I didn't want my tears to stop him from opening up. I held my crying boy for the next 40 minutes, sitting on the floor of our kitchen with my back resting on the refrigerator door. Every now and then he would muster up just a few quiet comments like "Why don't I get a sign?" or "I just want her back."

 My mom abundantly and unconditionally loved her grandchildren. You could see it on her face and on theirs when she was with them. You could feel it, hear it, almost touch it. In the past several months it was clear that her love amazingly still continued, even past the boundaries of life and death. And so, as we sat on the floor crying together, I did the only thing I could, I hoped desperately that somehow she could hear me, and I began to beg. I begged like a relentless two-year-old pleading for candy, for the entire time I held him. I begged my mom and I begged God to show him this endless love now: Mom, if you can hear me right now, give him a sign. Please, please, please. Mom, he *really* needs this. I will give up any sign you will ever give me in the future if you can just give him one—just one. An obvious, clear sign. Something just for him. Please Mom, please.

    Then I begged God: God, please, please, PLEASE. I don't know how this works but he needs a sign so badly. Please stop this pain inside him. God, let him know she's okay. God please help him when I cannot. There's nothing I can say or do; it is all you. Help this boy.

    After a colossal amount of silent screaming and begging, I hesitantly asked Logan if he wanted to pray with me. I was left with nothing else that could possibly help him. Part of me was hoping he would say no, in the case that his prayer would go unanswered and therefore seemingly unheard. He calmed down a bit though and replied yes. He wanted me to pray that he would receive a sign, just for him. I instantly put my guard up. Oh God, talk about setting him up for even more tears later. God, *please* answer this kid's prayer. I took another deep breath and I prayed with him cautiously, being very careful with my words. I feared he would feel forgotten again if his prayers were not clearly answered. Out loud, I asked vaguely for a sign, for something just for Logan, as he requested, but I worded it as ambiguously as possible. Inside, I prayed clearly and concisely for a sign so there would be no mistaking.

    The next morning, he woke up as if the previous evening of crying was long ago. He went on with his day and the next week like nothing had happened, not mentioning it again. Seven days passed, and the time on the kitchen floor was now fading in our memories. My efforts to continue the conversation with him never went anywhere, and I figured this was just as well. I doubted that my begging would actually be heard and didn't want him to be disappointed if nothing happened. Forgetting it seemed like the most hopeful, probable option.

    The following weekend, we were staying at my brother's house in North Carolina. I woke up shortly after the boys and came upstairs to say good morning. When I reached the top of the stairs, I could see Logan happily sitting on a chair playing with a toy. As soon as he saw me he looked at me with a glowing smile, and stated in peaceful excitement, "Mom, I had a dream.

Grandma was talking to me."

I thought back to our prayer a week ago. Phew, I thought, a dream with grandma. We will count it, no matter what it's about or if it's just a coincidence. He is content and that's all I want. I had an idea of the type of dream it would likely be. I expected a kid dream—something in his kid language, something that they would have usually done together like making chocolate chip pancakes or looking for little creatures in a creek.

I tried to reply calmly, "That's so great, Logan. What did she say?"

My superficial daydreams were quickly shattered though as Logan began to explain his actual dream. Shivers crept over my whole body while I listened. He talked about the dream calmly and certainly, so content with the conversation she had just had with him. He explained that he couldn't see her, he could only hear her voice. I found this unusual, as Logan is an extremely visual boy and had never told us about any solely audible dreams before.

He continued on matter of factly, as if it wasn't unusual at all that grandma was talking to him, like it was just another conversation to add to their list of many. The only difference was that in this case, she wasn't right in front of him, and they weren't talking about anything normal like Legos. Instead, she told him how she was doing.

He looked at me and started to talk in a way that felt more like he was relaying a message than describing a dream. "She said she's not sick anymore," he explained. "And she told me she's in heaven, and that heaven is really cool—really cool." He spoke with certainty and understanding, as if heaven was as cool to her as a toy store was to him. He paused, and his smile looked complete. I noticed how full he looked—fully happy and fully at peace.

I probably resembled more of a panting dog waiting for treats, wanting to hear the rest. "That's awesome Logan! Did she say anything else?" I had been taken off guard and left in a sea of curiosity. This was more than just a little kid's dream.

"Yea," he said, happily and nonchalantly. "She told me that she has met a lot of people."

"Woah," I said calmly, trying to stay as collected as he was being. "Did she say who?"

"No, she just said a lot of people. And she sounded really

happy mom!"

He went on to explain that her voice sounded like she was up above him a little bit, and like she was talking through a speaker "or something like that."

"Oh, neat! So you couldn't see her at all?"

"No, everything was just white. But she told me what she looked like."

I tried to stay calm, worried I would stop him from sharing. I wanted every detail though. I wanted to know what she looked like now too. "That's great! What did she say?"

"She told me that she was all white and had wings." He paused for a second and said in an excited but matter-of-fact tone, "She said that she is an angel now."

I blinked away a tear in my eye. It struck me how special this dream was, from the way he was telling it, from the differences in his normal dreams, from the simplicity but also the depth of the conversation. I told him that it sounded like an awesome dream.

He shook his head and smiled like he and grandma had a secret that I didn't quite get and then said "Mom, she was really talking right to me! It didn't feel like a regular dream, it just felt like she was talking to me."

"Logan, that is so awesome, buddy!"

He smiled and I was struck again by how content he looked.

"Hey Logan," I asked, as he headed toward the army men his brothers were now playing with. "Do you remember how you felt when Grandma was talking to you?" I thought this might be a long-shot question, maybe too abstract for him to pinpoint.

Instead, he stopped in mid army man grab, a giant smile covering his face, to the point where even his eyes were smiling. "I felt happier than I have ever felt in my whole life," he replied. He held the giant smile for a minute, and I smiled back. He turned back to the army men. His smile relaxed but it continued to hold a light again that had been dimmed for way too long.

Finding Hope

September 30, 2014

Then...Hope is essential, but also can make you feel very vulnerable. It can feel like setting yourself up for failure. If what you hoped for doesn't pan out, then what?

Now...Hope is essential, and can make you very vulnerable. Vulnerability leads to an openness that is necessary to move forward, and opens your eyes to see how hope may have transformed. It may not look exactly as you first expected, but it's still there in its own amazing way.

    A friend of mine asked me to write an essay about breast cancer and hope for an event she was hosting at her store. I was excited for the opportunity, as it had been a while since I even had a chance to relax, let alone write. Now was an especially needed time for this, as it had been one year since my mom first went to the hospital with the symptoms that would not be fixed.
    I went to one of my favorite places that we used to always go to with my mom and dad, our local Children's Lake. The lake is a beautiful spot that runs along the Appalachian Trail. We loved to bring our kids here to feed the ducks, climb trees, canoe, and hike. I found a spot away from people, as I knew whenever I wrote about my mom I could plan on tears as well.
    Pen and paper ready, I thought of the word hope—hope and cancer, cancer and hope. As I tossed these words around in my head, other words began to get louder, words I hadn't thought would be a part of the story I would write about hope. Instead, the

words in my mind were only the opposite: ugly, awful cancer, death, loss, grief, hopelessness. No hopeful words or stories came to my mind. I suddenly became almost disgusted at the word hope and had an overwhelming desire to make the word hope completely disappear. The only thing I felt when thinking of this word, "hope," was bitterness. Our family had stayed so hopeful, but the hope we clung to was unfulfilled in the way we most desperately wanted. My intention of writing a positive, uplifting story was now shattered, and instead, my head was a chorus of negativity. How could I write about hope when our hope for my mom to live was destroyed? I felt like anything I would write would be a lie for what I was truly feeling. If I was totally honest in this moment, this is what I would have written:

Hope: what a joke. Don't cling to this. We hoped and hoped and look what happened. No one wants to hear about hope from me. My story ends with loss, with death.

My mind flashed back and forth between the experiences we had that were full of hope and the huge sense of loss that hadn't gone away. My positive side fought courageously to win this battle, and my next thought was: *Yes, but we saw hope, we did, not in the way we expected, but it was there.* The battle raged on, and the next thing I knew I was back to Captain Negativity. *Yea, sure, we experienced some incredible things, but it wasn't like we had first wanted, not in the way we asked, begged, and pleaded.*

Then positivity tried to strike back. *We did see so much hope though, amazing hope we never expected—endless hope, eternal hope.*

It wasn't enough though, and one last punch of pain won this battle. *Yes, but is she here? No, and that's all that matters.*

By now, my eyes were completely bloodshot and I could feel the streaks of mascara smeared down my face. The unrelenting sun was blinding my already stinging eyes. I decided to put down my pen that hadn't even written a single letter and head to the car in hopes of finding a pair of sunglasses. I used my sleeve to wipe my cheeks and took deep breaths to attempt composure for the sake of any innocent strangers I might happen to pass.

I unlocked my door and searched the van for the much-needed shades. All I could find were two kid pairs, crusted with crackers and fingerprints. I decided to wipe them off and give them a try, but they were way too tight. I put them down and sat in the driver's seat, defeated. I decided to give it one last try before I went home, with no story and no hope. I checked through a bag and then around my oldest son's seat. No luck. I got out of the car, and looked under my seat, hoping a pair had fallen.

And there it was. Right there! Oh, God, there it was! I loudly laughed, cried, and screamed, all at the same time, no longer aware of anyone around. I said out loud with no hesitation, "Mom, I love you. Thank you Mom, thank you. I love you. I miss you. You are so hilarious! Thank you!" There, under my seat, where I and several others had thoroughly looked at least five times before was Logan's long-lost iPod.

Logan had been much more like himself for a couple of weeks following the dream with my mom, but over the past month, the rollercoaster of emotions was again in full swing. His previous even-keeled, easy-going personality had turned completely tumultuous. We tiptoed around him, never sure how he would react to even seemingly minor things. Any change and any loss since (even just stuff) had been a catastrophe. Two months ago, he lost his iPod, which he had saved his own money for and had taken many treasured pictures with, including several of his beloved grandma. There were pictures from our trip with her a month before she got sick, videos of us laughing and exploring together. We looked EVERYWHERE for this iPod, forming whole family search parties several times. We completely emptied the van twice, vacuumed every corner and every crevice, and searched under every single seat. We folded the seats down, back, forward, and removed every rug and seat we could. I never knew a van could get so gutted. The very spot it laid today had been checked thoroughly numerous times by numerous people, with no luck. We wanted this iPod not for the thing that it was, but for any bit of Logan's mind that it might help to settle.

Two nights ago, with Logan's emotions hitting an all-time low, I prayed desperately for God to intervene, and to carry him when I had tried everything and nothing had helped. I begged my mom again, despite how ridiculous it seemed. "Mom, please, if you can hear me, help him. Help him, please. Be with him. I want my sweet, loving boy back."

As I held the iPod in my hand, I laughed, again shaking my head, knowing somehow my prayer had been answered.

However it works, she is really still with him. As a mom I had tried everything to help him and felt inferior to the pain he was facing, as nothing I tried had worked. Being shown again that my husband and I were not the only ones helping him through this gave me more hope than I had felt in a long time. I stood in the parking lot laughing, with my face now completely soaked.

Feelings of incredible love, joy, and hope flooded my soul. Hope. My mom had found his lost iPod, and at the exact right time, handed me my lost hope. I could almost hear her say, "Don't ever lose hope, Kimberly, love will always win. You will get your sweet boy back soon." I smiled ear to ear and cried tears of joy as I headed back to the bench, with Logan's iPod, a pen, some paper, and an amazing feeling of boundless, radiant hope.

Finches

July 2015

Then...I guess you have to experience it to believe it.

Now...Even when you do actually experience it, you can still talk yourself out of it.

"Mom?" Logan said, looking up from his book.

"Yea, buddy" I replied, expecting a question or comment about the book he was reading.

"Why do some people say that a bird is a sign of a person who died?"

Okay, I thought to myself, a bit deeper than anything in *Captain Underpants*. I put down my soapy dish sponge and walked closer to him.

"Well, I think some people have certain birds that remind them of a person they lost, and some people think that a certain bird is sent from a loved one."

He looked at me with some sadness in his eyes. "Why don't we have a bird from Grandma?"

I thought for a moment, realizing the way I answer this could either help or hurt whatever he was trying to process. "Hmm, maybe because we have other signs like earrings or dreams? I'm not sure, buddy."

Not settled, he continued, "Well, if there *was* a bird for Grandma, what kind do you think it would be?"

I played along and said the first one that came to my mind.

109

"I think maybe it would be a goldfinch. They were one of her favorites."

By now, my other two boys had joined the conversation and wanted to see a picture of a goldfinch. We looked them up, talked for another minute or two, and seeming satisfied, they went back to their books. They didn't bring the topic back up, and neither did I.

A couple of weeks passed and I hadn't thought of the conversation much, if at all. Paul and I had had a few long, crazy days back-to-back. I decided to go run on my normal loop for a much-needed stress break. As I ran, I started praying about everything that was going on. It was my mom's birthday a few days before, and I felt my emotions creeping up in all the stress cracks that had been forming. I thought about how much better things would be if I just had her here—how much easier, how much happier. My eyes began to fill, my nose became stuffy, and breathing became increasingly difficult. I knew from my experience a while ago, crying and running do not mix well. I fought to control it and kept going. I tried to think about her in a less depressing way, mostly so I could keep running and not hyperventilate again. I tried focusing on the positive and the many things I was grateful for. I thought about what an awesome mom and grandma she was and what a great model I had to learn from. As these thoughts were streaming through my mind, a bright goldfinch flew right in front of me and landed a few feet ahead. It looked straight at me. Wow, that's neat, I thought, a goldfinch. Mom's favorite. I continued running. As I got closer to the bird, it flew just a few feet ahead, landed in front of me, and looked right at me again. It waited for my next step or two and then flew ahead again. I kept running, and the finch did this four more times, like it was playing. I thought about how excited my mom would be about this little finch.

As it finally flew away, my conversation with Logan came into mind…a bird as a sign? The rational side of my brain wrote it off quickly though, despite everything I had already experienced, and I passed it off as just an extremely friendly bird.

A few minutes later, I turned the corner and headed toward home. My mind and heart were battling again as I fought to hold my grief back so I could finish the run. Despite all my effort to stay positive, I kept going back to the thought of how much I needed her, and how hard life was without her here. I saw a few birds ahead but thought nothing of it. As I got a little closer, I realized they weren't just any bird, they were also goldfinches. Then I realized there were not just a few of them; there had to be at least 40 of them, flying all around. As I jogged along the side of the road, goldfinches were everywhere I looked: next to me, in front of me, behind me, far away, and within three feet of me. A couple of them flew around me as I ran, some in circles, some over my head. I had never seen anything like it on this very same route that I had run countless times.

    I stopped for a while and just watched them. I thought of the playful goldfinch a half-mile back. I thought of my response to it and the way I passed it off as nothing. And now, all of these finches, flying everywhere! I began to laugh right there on the side of the street, sweaty, crying, laughing, and bird-watching. My mom must have known how very clear I needed signs to be in order to believe them. One bird wouldn't do it, but 40 swarming finches would.

    When Logan came home, I gave him a huge hug. I pulled him into my arms and hugged him tightly. "Hey bud, I have a really cool story to tell you. I think Grandma was listening to our conversation a couple of weeks ago."

And More Finches...

April 2017

Then...Are these experiences anything that can impact other people, or just for our family?

Now...These experiences are meant to be shared in more ways than one.

      Her ashes had been sitting in the same spot for three years—in the perfect little box, sometimes in plain sight and sometimes covered with Luke's creations. I never liked having them there, but I couldn't think of any other place for them. I didn't want them in my room because I didn't want them to be the last thing I saw at night and the first thing I saw in the morning. Hidden didn't seem right either though. I contemplated burying them numerous times, but it just never felt right. I felt like it needed to be a planned out, grand event with music, readings, a pastor, etc., but I just couldn't get it together.
      My brothers and their families were all coming for Easter so I decided this would be the perfect time. I let everyone know months in advance that we would be burying them that weekend and I thought for sure I'd have time to pull a nice little ceremony together. Instead, it came down to the night before everyone was set to arrive, and I had not a single thing planned or prepared. I grabbed a piece of paper and forced myself to at least write something. I strongly considered postponing it, thinking maybe it just wasn't meant to be that weekend. I wrote about a page, which was almost entirely illegible, and ran out of time to finish.

A few days later as one of my brothers and his family were preparing to head home, I decided to just go for it. All I had was the one-page chicken scratch to read, but everyone was there and I had no idea when the next opportunity would be. Having the ashes just sitting on a desk amidst a pile of who knows what for another year felt worse than doing a hasty, semi ceremonial burial. I asked my husband quickly if he could grab a shovel, and I grabbed the ashes and the journal I had scratched the poem out on. I had not read it since I wrote it, but I figured it was better than the alternative: nothing.

We piled in our cars and drove to my mom's bench, a bench we had bought in her honor with her name on it and a quote from that fateful December night years before, "Love is everywhere if you look for it." The bench was only a half-mile from our house, in a beautiful park we spent time at regularly. There was a baseball field in front of it where our family would go and play together, and a field to the left that always had majestic sunsets. It was the only appropriate spot I could think of, so there we were. The burial was simple but nice, with each of us saying something about her and putting a wildflower we had picked into the hole. I attempted to read the poem the best I could, between tears and some completely illegible words. We ended it with a prayer, good tears, and hugs.

The following week was filled with crazy days of getting back into the swing of things after almost a week of fun with family. I hadn't been back to the bench yet. I had 30 minutes to run one day, so I decided to head to the bench and stretch there like usual. As soon as I got to it, I started to get choked up thinking about the significance of the spot now and missing her. I sat down on the bench holding back tears and looked out toward the park. I thought about how thankful I was that we had a place like this to remember her. I was also thinking how great it would be if we could help put in a bench for a family we knew whose mom passed away a couple of years ago, leaving behind a husband and six children under 18. As I was thinking this thought, not even there for a minute yet, I saw something yellow flash by. I instantly teared up. There, flying right in front of me, was a goldfinch! It flew to the tree right next to her bench, landed and looked right at me, and started loudly singing. It sang for about two minutes, then flew away while I was videotaping it.

By now with all the things my family had experienced since she died, I had no hesitation this little finch was a sign from my mom. It was just too much to be anything else. The fact that it was my first time back to the bench since we buried her ashes, along with my uncertainty about burying them, and that I had not seen a single goldfinch at that park in almost three years, was just too much to shrug off. Then there also was the thought I was having the moment a finch came flying by, that another family needed a bench as well. It was a thought that my mom would have loved and supported. It was a thought I believe she wanted to happen, signaling with the sign of a little yellow bird. Yes, she's happy with her spot. Yes, she's happy with the idea. Yes, she is so happy she could sing.

Two weeks later, I began a fundraiser for the bench for the family, just a few days before Mother's Day. In a day and a half, $1,037 was raised to fully cover the cost of the bench. I let the father of the family know the good news and he was very excited and thankful. Later that day, I went for a run in our neighborhood. As I ran, a goldfinch flew right in front of me, beautiful and bright. I smiled but didn't think too much of it until I realized where I was. The moment it flew by, I was right in front of this family's house! This bright little bird was the exclamation mark at the end of this story, a story that felt even more special because it involved people outside of my own family. These signs always felt personal, but the fact they could also be used to bless someone else filled me with even more awe than usual.

Whale-watching Flop
July 5, 2017

Then...After all we have experienced you would think I wouldn't be surprised when signs of my mom occur.

Now...I am still surprised, each and every time.

    My brothers and I and our families went on a beautiful trip to Banff National Park and Squamish, British Columbia. We planned to finish the trip off with a whale-watching tour to see orcas around the San Juan Islands in Washington state. Spotting whales had become an infatuation of mine, and I was so excited to share this experience with everyone.
    The night before, my husband and I brought my niece and nephew to our Airbnb so that my brothers and their wives could spend the evening in Vancouver. We planned to meet the next morning at the whale-watching dock, bright and early.
    Paul and I got the five kids up and out the door with a few minutes to spare. We started driving and called my brothers to see if they made it out the door as scheduled. They were about four minutes ahead of us. Perfect! Everything was going as planned for this last day of our trip. Our GPS was saying we should arrive 30 minutes before the boat was scheduled to leave, just as they recommended.
    As we drove, I told the kids all about the majestic creatures we were about to see. I showed them pictures on my phone and their faces lit up with excitement. My niece and nephew had never

seen whales before and had been talking about this moment for weeks.

Halfway into our one-hour drive to the dock, we saw many red brake lights ahead of us. Suddenly, ours were on too, and we found ourselves parked two minutes later in the middle of the interstate. As some more time went by, people started to get out of their cars to see what the hold-up was. Through the grapevine, we found out a bad accident had occurred just a football field in front of us, and that the person was going to be life-flighted out.

We all said prayers for the person, and then our own selfish panic sunk in. We were stuck on the highway, with no way of knowing how long we would be stopped. There was no way off the highway. The minutes ticked away as our car sat parked. We called my brothers to check in and see where they were, and fortunately they had missed the accident by a couple of minutes. We made a plan that they would continue on, and beg the boat to wait for us. Each family had spent hundreds of dollars on these tickets, so we thought surely there would be some grace period.

About 10 minutes later my brothers called back. They had done a lot of begging, but the boat crew said they could only wait five minutes and no longer. There was just no way it was going to happen. We decided we would try to get our money back and then find another company with a later departure. If we couldn't get our money back though, there was no way any of us would be able to afford another company. This was the grand hoorah at the end of our trip, already spending way more than we normally would on any one adventure.

My sister-in-law called back and said the company was insisting they would not refund us and could only give us a raincheck for another day. The fact that we lived on the other side of the country and were leaving tomorrow seemed to be factors that didn't phase them as problems. Paul and I and the kids sat in our parked car in the middle of a highway, full of frustration and disappointment. How would we tell these five little kids that whale watching wasn't going to happen?

A few minutes later, a mercy flight helicopter landed not far in front of us. I felt shallow. I had been raging about our own situation when someone else just a hundred yards from us had just been critically injured, or worse. I calmed down and broke the news to the kids as they watched the helicopter that we likely will not be able to see the whales.

The cars began to move shortly after and 10 minutes into driving, now only 20 minutes away, my brothers and sister-in-laws Facetimed us to watch the boat pull away. We laughed sadly and told them we'd be there soon. We hadn't found another company yet, or convinced the current one of a refund, but at least we were on our way now.

We pulled up to the building by the dock where everyone had been waiting for us. We all hugged when we walked in, feeling like we had just been through a marathon of disappointment. As we embraced, a song came on in the background that changed the mood instantly. It was "Somewhere Over the Rainbow," one of my mom's favorite songs. We had played it many times in her last few days. We all felt a little lighter and a little more hopeful. A moment later, I looked over at Luke to see him smiling ear to ear. He was holding up three coins that he'd found on the ground right in front of him—three coins right where my brothers and their wives had been standing for an hour waiting for us, but no one had seen them. "It's going to be okay," he said to me smiling, "Grandma is here, mom."

We laughed together and relaxed in the beauty of the moment. My mom would have loved this vacation. She would have loved every moment of the family being together and every bit of adventure we had planned. Also, in this situation, she would have persevered and made it happen.

We got on our phones, and my brother went back to the company's office to try to get our money back. Within 10 minutes, we had all of our money back and had scheduled a tour with a different company for later that morning. We all celebrated. We drove 20 minutes away, did the tour with a terrific company, and saw tons of orcas. To top it off, this trip was even better than the first one would have been, now knowing that my mom was with us too.

A Little Bit of Them All

August 2017

Then…Some things you have to do in life are so hard, so painful, and just plain suck.

Now…These things are a lot easier when you know you are not alone.

  I loved the house we had built six years ago. I loved everything about it, and in fact, to this day I still do. My husband and I designed it, considering every little detail. Countless memories were made in this house, and I loved knowing that memories of my mom lived in this house as well. I could remember playing endless games of spades in our kitchen, dying Easter eggs with the boys, and coming down the stairs to the smell of pancakes and my mom cooking, with one kid on the counter helping, snacking on a chocolate chip. I could picture my boys waiting eagerly by the front window for my mom and dad to pull into the driveway, ready to run out and jump into their arms. I could look out the back door and remember her pushing the kids on the swings, flipping rocks to look for bugs with the boys, playing backyard baseball, and celebrating countless birthdays on the back patio.
  We faced a continuous challenge with this beloved house, however. The situation with one of our neighbors was very volatile, and our kids (and Paul and I) no longer felt comfortable in our own yard. After years of dealing with this and trying everything we could, a couple of incidents put the icing on the cake. We knew the

time had come to really consider leaving the house we built. Realizing it wasn't going to be easy emotionally, financially, or logistically, Paul and I said to each other that if this was what we really needed to do, God was going to have to pretty much hand us our next house. It would have to be clear that it was what we needed to do, as we loved our house and knew it wouldn't be easy to let it go. We loved our neighborhood and we loved so many things about our house that we were going to be quite picky moving to another house. We basically decided that it would have to be one of the 10 houses that backed up to a park in our neighborhood. The kids would still have all their friends nearby, and we'd have plenty of room to kick soccer balls and play baseball.

In May, we got a call from a friend who said that she had this persistent feeling that God wanted her to let us buy the house her family was planning on buying and were currently living in. They were renting the house and had convinced the landlord to sell it to them and were only a few days away from closing. She said she just couldn't shake the feeling that it was not their house and should actually be ours. She knew the situation we were in with our neighbor but didn't know if we were ready to move. As soon as she began talking, I knew we were getting our answer. A house was being handed to us, and go figure—it was one of the 10 houses we always talked about.

The purchase of this new house went smoothly, and our current house sold right away. All seemed like it was going well, which is why I was so surprised when the emotions hit me like a ton of bricks. I had been wrestling back and forth, but usually the feelings of excitement and relief won over the bad feelings. As moving day approached though, I began to lose all composure. This was our house that we built with love, that we built to raise our boys in, that was filled with memories, and now it felt like we were being forced out. Moving wasn't what we wanted to do but was what we needed to do for the safety and peace of our family. It felt like we were being defeated by hate, and like the home we all loved was being taken from us. The new house felt foreign and empty; there were no memories, no love—just empty.

A couple of days before our big move was to take place, the boys and I went over to the new house for the first time since our friends had moved out. Luke ran in first, followed by the other boys. He ran into the living room to check out his new house and then turned to me excitedly. "Look, Mom!" he yelled. "A penny!" He smiled ear to ear as he held the penny up proudly for me to see. "Grandma likes our house, Mom," he said matter of fact, and then ran upstairs to see his new room. I laughed and shook my head, thinking how cool it was that there just happened to be a penny laying right in the middle of the floor in this completely empty house. This comforted me momentarily, but the unsettled, displaced feelings came back quickly once I started to walk around the house. I only could find things I didn't like, as if I had blinders on and couldn't see all the good.

    My husband started some of the remodeling on the new house, and moving day came a couple of days later, in the middle of the construction zone our new house had become. We had at least 20 people helping us. Every box my friends carried out of the truck, I wanted it to go right back into our old house. I never actually took a box back into the house, but I envisioned it numerous times. I don't think I looked a single friend in the eye the whole time. I was afraid if I did, they would notice the sadness, ask me about it, and then I'd let all the tears flow.

    Somehow the move was complete later that day, and all of our belongings were now scattered chaotically amidst this strange new house. We had boxes and boxes filled with stuff, covering the half torn out carpet upstairs and piled to the ceiling in the office, as the rest of the downstairs floor had also been torn out. Drywall dust coated everything from the wall my husband had knocked out the day before. Walking into this "new house" felt ugly, chaotic, and painful.

    My friends stayed for a while that evening, half to help and half because they could sense I was on the verge of completely losing it. I was walking around aimlessly, trying hard not to break down completely, when my friends called me into my backyard. "Kim, you have to see this!"

    I stepped outside to see them pointing to two goldfinches, happily flying about in our backyard, singing their song. I smiled for the first real smile all day.

    The next morning I told my friend who had just been living at this house about the finches. She said she sat outside on the back deck almost every day for the last two years in the warm weather and had never once had seen a goldfinch anywhere around. The rest of the day continued on like the day before: chaotic, loud, and unsettling. I tried to focus on the positive, on how clear it was that this house was meant for us, on how the kids could play outside with no fear, but my emotions felt like weights holding down any joy. I attempted to put the kids to bed while Paul continued to work tirelessly on the renovations. He was fully aware that I was a ticking time bomb.

One of the boys needed a fan for his room, so I mustered up all the energy I had left for this one task and walked downstairs to look for it. I was so close to bursting, it was scary. I have never had a panic attack before, but I imagine I was on the verge. I couldn't think clear thoughts and had to repeatedly say *fan, fan, fan* in my head, as my brain barely had the capacity for even this one minor task.

I did not have any luck in the office, which was where we piled everything that didn't have a place yet, so I headed to the garage, with tears about to burst directly out of my brain. I opened the door and saw something lying there, right in front of me. It was not a fan; it was way better. My emotions exploded, but not out of stress this time. There, lying in the middle of the pathway, was one, lone shiny earring! I fell to my knees, and the stress that had been strangling me instantly released its grip. It was going to be okay.

The coin, the finch, and now the earring—all in the last three days, all at pivotal breaking points. In our first few days in this house that my mom will never actually walk into, the very first memories were of her. I smiled, now only my second real smile in the last few days. It was clear…it was going to be okay. Our family was meant to be in this house; God arranged and Mom approved.

Grandma Dottie

February 3, 2018

Then...Maybe these things are only particular to my mom for some reason? I had never really heard stories like this before, could it happen with other lost loved ones?

Now...Love wins: across time, across people, across places...love always wins.

    My Grandma Dottie, my mom's mom, was the picturesque grandma inside and out. She never stood more than five feet tall, even in her younger years, and near the end of her life she was under four-and-a-half feet tall. Her hair was as white and plush as cotton, with soft curls that had been set with rollers each morning. She baked cinnamon rolls that no matter how well she explained the recipe, no one could make them quite like hers. She played cards, knowing the rules to an unbelievable amount of games, and played each game like there was a heaping pot of money riding on it. She remembered every single birthday and sent a card even when her hands challenged her to write. She remembered stories and experiences, some dating back to as early as four years old....88 years of memories!
    In January 2018, she developed pneumonia, which led to complications including congestive heart failure. At 92, pneumonia can be very serious. When my grandma was first brought to the ER, she was unresponsive upon arrival. Her condition continued to decline, and she remained unresponsive for days. The doctors did not think she would wake up again and estimated it would be a

few hours to a few days maximum until she passed away. My oldest son Jake and I hopped in the car to drive to New York, all too reminiscent of the years before when we made this drive for my mom. About an hour from the hospital, my dad called and wanted to know how far away we were. Despite the doctor's prediction, she had woken up and was talking to all our family that surrounded her. My dad said to hurry, as she was in pain and they were waiting to give her morphine until everyone had said goodbye. They knew this would be the last chance to talk to her. I was thankful that Jake was in the car, as it kept me at a safer speed than I wanted to drive. We parked quickly and ran into the hospital and up the stairs to her floor.

When we walked in, she smiled and turned to us, and with the same happy and surprised tone she had each time I called, said, "Oh, hi Kimberly!" It instantly brought tears to my eyes, knowing how much I would miss that voice, that excitement upon my arrival. She then saw Jake standing a little behind me, and a tear welled in her eye as he came over and gave her a hug.

Each of her family members were able to come to the hospital or do a video call with her to tell her how much they loved her, how much she meant to them, and to say goodbye. She mustered up the energy to tell each person she loved them and to hold her husband's hand. She even had enough energy to tell her husband what to do, including that he better get a drink because he must be thirsty. The only person she did not get to say goodbye to was my cousin, Josh. He was driving straight through from Florida to try to make it to the hospital to say goodbye in person. She held off on the pain medicine for as long as possible but couldn't take it any longer. Late that afternoon, the nurses came in with ample medicine, and she fell asleep for what we thought would be one last time. We waited with her for a while, as any moment at this point could be the last. Hours passed though, and her vitals were holding stable. Most of us left the hospital, as visiting hours were over, and then waited by the phone for the imminent call. We didn't get one though, not until the next morning around 9 a.m.

My cousin had driven nonstop and arrived around 8:45 a.m. He sat beside her and held her hand as he told her he loved her. Just a few minutes later, she took her final breath. She had clearly waited for him, waited for the last loved one to have a chance to say goodbye. Grandma Dottie never left anyone out, and she didn't let death do this either.

    Her funeral was beautiful. I smiled as the people walked in, filling every spot in the church. She would have been very humbled by this and wondered why people would "make such a fuss" about her. I read a poem I wrote, my cousin read a story, and another cousin sang the song: "I Can Only Imagine." It was the same song my mom had chosen for her funeral and my grandma had been very moved by it, so she requested it as well.

    Our family headed home to Pennsylvania after the funeral. It was late, so we unpacked quickly and went upstairs, huddling in the hallway like usual to read a book and pray together before bed. I picked up a random dusty book on our shelf and began reading; it was a true story about doctors who spent 25 hours straight in surgery disconnecting twins who were joined at the head. The story talked about the complete exhaustion the doctors felt. During the surgery, the doctors believed something supernatural had to have been leading their hands when they didn't feel like they could move them anymore. They said what they did was beyond their human capabilities. The exact moment the doctors got the very last blood vessels separated, the choir song "Hallelujah" came on their radio. All the doctors got chills and knew for sure they had not been alone in that operating room.

    We all thought it was a really neat story, so we looked it up online and watched a few minutes of a video describing more of what happened. When it ended, we began to reminisce about all the miracles that had happened with my mom and the many events we experienced that just could not be explained. Then we started to pray together as we did each night. It had been an exhausting week, and an even more exhausting day with my grandma's funeral, luncheon, burial, and a six-hour drive home—all in 13 hours—but I tried to pull myself together to decide what I really wanted to say to God as I prayed. The feelings that came to me most, whenever I thought of my grandma, were love and gratitude. I began to pray with the boys and thanked God for my Grandma Dottie. I thanked him for all our amazing memories with her, and for the incredible person she was. Then, I thanked God that she was in heaven with him. Despite how much I already missed her, I knew she was incredibly happy now—happy beyond our understanding. The very moment I said this, I heard something that made me instantly freeze. The boys, Paul, and I exchanged looks, but nobody spoke; they were frozen as well. The moment after I thanked God for my grandma being in heaven, the very song she chose for her funeral, the song we cried to just hours before, the song my mom had chosen as well, the song that talked about how beautiful heaven would be, came on the stereo downstairs! We had been playing Pandora before we brought the kids up for bed and forgot to turn it off. Not only was it the song she chose, but it was also just like the miracle we had researched and read about one minute before, with music being the medium through which a spiritual connection was made, the moment following the end of something significant.

No one said a word for the first minute; we all just continued to look at each other with wide eyes. The five of us all knew that what just happened was no coincidence. One of the boys then broke the ice with a hesitant comment, "Umm, this is really weird." We all laughed, shaking our heads, and sat in amazement, listening to this song, wondering how this could possibly happen. We all sat and listened to the song "I Can Only Imagine" in awe, covered with smiles and goosebumps. For another time that day, and for so many times in the past few years, painful but thankful tears rolled down cheeks.

The boys had started finishing their bedtime routine, but I continued to sit in the hallway, as thoughts and questions filled my mind. Before this moment, I had thought these connections were exclusive to my mom, but now they were happening with my grandma too? My mind began to open to what this could all mean, to people outside of just our family. What if we all knew there was so much more happening around us than we could possibly understand? What if we took off the skeptic lenses, similar to the ones I wore so tightly for so long, and instead freely enjoyed the gifts before us? What if we all lived knowing that death is not the end of the story? What if we all lived knowing that in the end, love always wins?

Two Little Gifts

December 29, 2020

Then...Over three years have gone by since anyone had experienced a sign from my mom. Maybe over time these connections end for some reason?

Now...Love truly has no boundaries.

  The year 2020 gave everyone a story. There were countless stories of loss and grief, division, loneliness, economic hardship, anxiety, and pain unlike many have experienced before. There were also stories of triumph, victorious love, families figuring out how to spend time with each other again, and healing. The year 2020 brought my family both the positive and negative, but it also gave us something completely unexpected: two little girls and another chapter of The Story.
  Shortly after my mom passed away, my awareness of other people who lost loved ones was heightened, especially of children who had lost a parent. I felt compelled to help in some way, to somehow help ease the pain they were going through. This led me to think about foster children, and the tragic situations they experience as their "normal." Foster children are often removed from their parents just like in the movies, including filling the classic trash bag with their belongings, and an hour later, moving into a new home with complete strangers. The trauma they face in being displaced and losing everything they know, including whatever trauma they are being removed from, is more than most people can even bear to imagine. This population of children

began to fill my mind daily, and the desire to give these children all the love I could in whatever time they would be with me became increasingly strong. I started to share this with my husband, and after lots of thought and conversation, the idea slowly began to settle in for him too.

After about eight months of training and paperwork, our family was officially approved to foster children on February 12, 2020. The next day, we got our first call about a possible placement. The caseworker explained there were two little girls, ages three and four, one of them with significant behavioral needs. The girls were homeless and the mom was unable to provide what they needed. We hung up the phone, discussed it with our boys, and called back and told her that yes, we would like to be considered to take them. Since these girls were in a county one hour away, we didn't put all that much weight into saying yes, as we didn't think we would be chosen. Friends who were also fostering had been called for potential placements and then not chosen repeatedly due to proximity. The distance, however, apparently did not matter to the county workers in this case, as we got a call the next day that our family was chosen for these girls… and they would be at our doorstep in two hours!

Friends showed up within 10 minutes of my SOS going out, and within an hour, we had ample clothing, beds with princess comforters, girl toys that looked so unusual in our house, car seats, and a lot of anxiety and nerves. We watched as the car pulled up to our driveway, and two beautiful little girls hopped out. They both walked into our house without hesitation. Due to their past experiences, and already having been in foster care for over two years of their little lives, they had some obvious attachment, boundary, and behavioral issues. Within an hour of them being at our house, I began putting my behavior analysis background to work with the first goals entirely safety-based. They didn't respond to their names when called, didn't have any safety awareness, and would run blindly across a street, climb up bookcases, get into all the things they shouldn't (thankfully all medicine was locked up), run up and hug complete strangers, and the list goes on.

The next month of 2020 was a complete blur as it required everything we had mentally, physically, spiritually, and emotionally. To top it off, Paul also had a much-needed surgery on his foot a week after their arrival that required him to be bedridden for two weeks, with a boot and external pin for six additional weeks. Then, just as he began to hobble around and life seemed like we may possibly begin to manage it all again, the pandemic happened.

For the girls, and for our family's relationship with them, the initial several months of shutdown ended up being a tremendous gift. We were able to spend ample time giving them the attention they needed without the numerous distractions daily life can bring. We were able to bond with them to a level that would have taken significantly longer. As we spent every minute of every day with them for months and months, we were able to clearly see their skills and their needs, and we worked to build a solid foundation of trust and growth.

In the summer of 2020, the language of the county caseworkers began to change. The girls initially were supposed to only be with us for one or two months, and then COVID-19 happened, so it was expected for the time to be slightly longer. Six months later, however, the caseworkers began to question if their biological mom would ever be able to meet her goals in order for reunification to occur. One August morning, the caseworker called me and asked if our family would be open to adopting them if it came to that. I was speechless at first, completely taken off guard, as we had only planned on being foster parents and thought for sure the girls would be going back to their mom. I explained to the caseworker what our initial intentions were and that we would begin to consider this option.

For the next few weeks, Paul and I were like deer in headlights over this possibility. We attempted numerous times to begin talking about it, but words never came out. Prior to this, we had always been able to make decisions together successfully, but this was one of the most life-changing decisions we could possibly make, and not just for us but for the three boys and two girls too. In the past, all the decisions we have made were flexible in some way: buying a house—you can always sell and find a new one; changing jobs—you can always change again; moving to a new town—you can always move again. Adopting two children and the changes that it makes on your entire family dynamics and your future—there are no take backs; it is the real deal of decision-making.

In September and October 2020, the county increased the pressure on Paul and I to make a decision. While the hearing for termination of parental rights would not be for many months still, we were being asked each time the caseworkers visited our house. We decided to set up some conversations with the people who knew our family best, as well as people who have been in a similar situation, just to help get the conversation between Paul and I even started. We talked and prayed with our closest friends, met with our pastor and his wife who had both adopted and fostered, talked it over with our family, and basically brought it up to everyone we could think of who might possibly be helpful. We brought up our fears and hopes of each option, including the impact it could have on our biological kids and our marriage if we were not all on the same page. I shared that this was particularly a lot for one of our boys, and my concern was that saying yes to the girls would be saying no to him. I shared that if God somehow changes his heart, then it would make it quite clear what God wanted us to do, as that seemed like a nearly impossible feat. After a few weeks of long conversations, prayer, and inner turmoil, we realized there was one overwhelming theme from each discussion we had: we were not ready to make this decision yet. It didn't mean no, it didn't mean yes, it just meant *not right now*. Our family was not on the same page, with some of us ready and some of us not at all. Not making the decision yet was the one thing we could actually agree on.

For the next two months, we didn't talk more than a sentence a week about it. We were content to patiently sit in the unknown, and content to release the pressure that was attempting to crush us. Christmas time came quickly, and we filled our days focusing on our family and the present. It was a Christmas so different from the year prior, but so beautiful in many ways. We watched our boys experience so much joy in sharing their Christmas time and traditions with the girls. We watched the girls' faces light up as they made gingerbread houses, cut paper snowflakes, frosted cookies, caroled for neighbors, and opened their gifts.

A few days after Christmas, Paul and I had a rare opportunity to take a hike together, alone. We decided to take advantage of it and finally attempt the conversation about adoption again. The hike was cold, but beautiful, as we walked briskly along a ridge on the Appalachian Trail. We laid out the possible outcomes of both options and how those two options could play out. We laid out what would change, and what changes we were willing to accept and not accept. At the end of the conversation, while nothing quite earth-shattering was said, we both were, for the first time, leaning much closer toward yes.

When we got back into our car, we checked our phones, and both Paul and I had a missed call from the county caseworker. I called her back on our drive home, and she stated she would like our answer by the end of the week, not months like they had said. She was retiring at the end of the week and wanted to have the plan for the girls figured out ahead of time for the next hearing. She also told us that if we say no, there is another family that just contacted them. It was the foster family the girls were with as babies, who were willing to adopt them instead. I hung up the phone in shock, as the deadline was moved up so suddenly, but also because this was the first we had ever heard of anyone having contact with the previous foster family. I had asked each caseworker for many months to try to find any details about this family in order to help provide more understanding and context about the two years of the girl's lives, but no one was able to get ahold of any information about them. The girls had no memory of them, and it just felt so sad that there were over two years of their lives missing. For this connection to be made now gave both Paul and I an unsettled, confused feeling.

The boys were all hanging out in the kitchen when we got home and the girls were at preschool, so Paul and I seized the opportunity to continue the conversation with them and explain all that had transpired in the last few hours. I began sharing what we discussed and was cautious with my words knowing that the last time we talked to our boys about this, months ago, they were not all where Paul and I ended up today. We didn't want to force anyone into thinking any certain way, and so we both chose our words carefully in order to leave the conversation open. We then turned to the boys and asked them what they were feeling and their thoughts on adopting the girls. Logan was fully on board as he had been from the start. Luke hadn't put a lot of thought into it, as he was 12 and still readily living in the moment, but declared he was content with the direction. Then it was Jake's turn. He put his head slightly down and shook it, with a slight smile on his face, and then for the first time he had ever voiced any change in heart whatsoever, said "I don't think that other family is meant to have them. I think we are meant to adopt them."

Time froze briefly as we all processed what he said. His heart had somehow changed in these last two months. Our prayer for God to show us through this change had been answered! I held back tears as I told Jake that myself and many others had secretly been praying that if this is meant to be, our family will be unified in the decision. A huge part of this unity was his heart being changed from a black and white, no, not what we signed up for, to an openness that only God could create. Tears welled in his eyes and we hugged, revelling in the quiet movement that took place while we rested our minds for those two months.

When we picked the girls up from preschool that afternoon, Gabriella was in an ultra-funny mood, making us laugh regularly with each thing she said. Sabrina was feeling a little sick and was hilariously thankful for each little thing. If she dropped something and we picked it up, her response was elaborate and sincere. "Oh, thank you sooo much for doing that," she said, giving a giant five-year-old hug. She must have thanked us each three times for little, random reasons that would typically go ignored.

We had not spoken about any of our decisions with the girls, as it would not be helpful to them until everything was definite. They still had no idea that adoption was even a possibility. But after dinner, something else happened that felt like confirmation we were headed in the right direction. I was helping Gabriella brush her hair and she turned to me out of nowhere and said "Mommy (she had just started calling me mommy in the last few weeks), I love you so much. I really miss you when I'm with my other mommy. I want to live with you guys forever." Up until this point of living with us for ten and a half months, neither she nor her sister had ever said anything about wanting to live with us forever. On this day though, the day that for the first time the rest of us were secretly unified, her soul was also aligned.

The following morning, Paul and I both felt a weight on us, knowing that yesterday started the likely trajectory of a whole new normal. While the day before had been a beautiful day with a lot of things lining up showing us the way, today felt heavy. We checked in with the boys at lunchtime again to see how they were feeling, and they all still stood by their decision. I was proud and even a bit envious of their confidence. While so much added up throughout the day yesterday, fears and unknowns so quickly begin to seep in and try to steal the peace and joy right out from under us. Logan and Luke went to the basement to play video games, and Jake, Paul, and I decided to play a board game, Settlers of Catan. My mind was not fully there though as it began to wander and question worst-case scenarios.

As I sat down, I thought about the day before, and how quickly the time frame changed from March until the end of this week. Then it hit me... *The end of this week.* My mind began to race as I realized what the end of this week was. It was January 1, the anniversary of my mom's death. The day that made this all come to be, including fostering the girls from the start. Without my mom dying, I would not have had such an understanding of what it is like to not have your mom with you, to feel so lost and alone. I would not have had the desire I experienced after her loss to become a foster parent and give children the love of a mom and dad and family, for whatever time they were with us. We would not have these girls. What are the chances that this timeframe would suddenly change yesterday, and our deadline would change to the day that she died? How could this be so incredible, again? It had been years since my last sign of my mom working in my life, and I never dreamed of nor expected anything more.

As these thoughts flowed through my mind, I began to share them with Paul and Jake. "You know what is completely crazy, the end of the..." and then I stopped suddenly in my tracks. In the middle of my sentence, a song came on our Alexa that made nothing come out of my mouth except for "Holy S***" at least five times in a row. It was the very song that was played at her retirement party in the hospice center, sung at her funeral, and the very song I had clung to each time my heart ached from missing her. It was a song I hadn't heard in at least a year. There, in the middle of my sentence about the deadline of our decision being on such a significant day, the song "I Can Only Imagine" began to play.

I filled Paul and Jake in, and we all sat in awe. The memory came back to me of the doctor's office many years before, as my mom and I sat across from each other and the doctor laid out her prognosis. Without even speaking a word, we knew we were on the same page, even with the heaviness of his message. Today, seven years following her death, she somehow was able to break through all barriers to give her nod of approval for this monumental decision, and give me one more chapter of The Story.

There are certain things that are beyond us. This decision was beyond myself and my family. Today, and every day of my life, I will be grateful that there is more beyond us leading our way when we cannot find our paths alone. Thanks, God. Thanks, Mom.

Data

Then... There is nothing emptier than death, nothing more painful than death, nothing more permanent than death.

Now...Death is so painful. Despite this pain though, something even more powerful exists: love. Love defies all odds and breaks through the boundaries of life and death. It is boundless, eternal, and sometimes, just completely unexplainable.

    A pastor friend of ours once told me (after many years of my husband and I peppering him with questions and trying to find answers about things we didn't understand about God) that eventually you just have to accept that you are not going to get all the answers and take a leap of faith. Throughout The Story I was given, I was forced out of my comfort zone of my own thoughts and beliefs. I was continuously drawn back to believe the unbelievable. I was shown over and over that no, all my questions would not be answered, because there are things our minds just cannot fully understand. The more I have come to know God over the past few years, the more I have realized, wouldn't I want it this way? Would I really want to be able to fully comprehend God? Would I really want God to be that simple that my mind could fully understand him?
    Each event that happened in The Story was unpredictable and unexpected. There were many dark days when I hoped something amazing would happen, days when I felt I needed it most, but the experiences in The Story seemed to always happen

when I wasn't even in the state of mind to be able to hope for it. Once some unexplainable things began to happen, I started to think, Okay God, but is this just going to happen only to me, or to other people too? I wondered if these things would happen just to Christians, or to nonbelievers as well. And then it happened: The Story unfolded across people, across settings, across faiths—just what my scientific side needed. While I never got a specific label saying, "Kim, this is a sign" or "Kim, this is a miracle," it was pretty darn close. Then, it went beyond even what I asked for, with the unexplainable happening after my grandma's death too.

God gave me the data I needed to break through the walls I had built over time. God came alongside me on that leap of faith our friend talked about and showed me some of his incredible love at the same time. Despite my skepticism, I was shown repeatedly that death is not where the story ends. Death is only a beginning of something else, something beyond our wildest imaginations. It is the beginning of something so beautiful and so full of joy that our earthly brains cannot even comprehend it. Death is a beginning to somewhere "beautiful, beautiful, the best thing," as my mom had said.

I have realized that it does not matter how many times a miracle happens though, you still don't get used to it. It doesn't become normal, it becomes only what it is—a miracle. Miracles have no worldly explanations. Miracles are out of our control, outside of our understanding. Before The Story occurred, I wasn't okay with that. I needed facts, I needed to see it to believe it. I used to explain things away as coincidences. I could come up with explanations for other people's stories or conclude that it was very good timing. Eventually though, seeing all these things as a coincidence became way more absurd than seeing it as a miracle. There was just too much evidence and too much data showing these events were truly connected to something way beyond human capabilities. When we open our eyes to the beauty and the miracles God places all around us, we allow love to win. Light begins to seep into the darkest places, and we see that there is a way out. There is a way to experience joy in the most unlikely places.

The quote from my mom, or from God through my mom, "Love is everywhere if you look for it," resonates so often in my mind. There are many moments when I feel like love has lost, when situations seem too bleak, tragic, or hopeless that there is no way love can be found in it. When I remember the truth though, I realize it's not that love wasn't there; it's that I wasn't open to seeing it. When we begin to remove the blinders of skepticism, pain, loss, and suffering, we can begin to see the miracles around us that could otherwise go unnoticed. We can open our minds to the truth that no matter how hard we try to figure everything out, some things are just beyond us. We can begin to see this world is not the end, death is not the end, and the story doesn't end here. We can begin to see even in the hardest circumstances with boundaries that seem impossible to break through, love is still triumphant. Pain once again loses, and love continues to win.

Made in the USA
Middletown, DE
13 April 2022